# Setup for a Breakthrough—
# The Life of Joseph

"Darnell nailed it in *Setup for a Breakthrough*! This is a must-read if you are struggling to forgive. You'll gain new insights on the seasons in Joseph's life and lessons you can apply in your journey from disappointment to the fulfillment of God's promise."

**—Pastor Rod Loy, Lead Pastor**
First Assembly of God, North Little Rock, AR

"Bishop Darnell K. Williams is very much possessive of esteemed episcopal dignity, astute ecclesiastical and theological knowledge and practices, and impeccable Christian character and integrity. He now in *Setup for a Breakthrough—The Life of Joseph* once more continues to exemplify excellent servant leadership skills as well as the character attributes of humility, innovation, and accountability."

**—Archbishop Jason E. Owen**
Ecumenical Patriarch/Metropolitan

"Life seems to be unfair at times, and it can appear that God is silent during our most difficult moments. In his book, *Setup for a Breakthrough—The Life of Joseph*, Dr. Williams uses the uniqueness of the life of Joseph to show how God can use the many challenges we experience to bring fulfillment to His purposes and our dreams. A must read for every Christian leader in the trenches of life and ministry."

**—Dr. Pat P. Glasgow**
Lead Pastor, La Horquetta Gospel Foundation, Trinidad
General Bishop, Pentecostal Assemblies of the West Indies
President of the West Indies School of Theology

"The biblical in-depth research that Dr. Darnell Williams has done on the life of Joseph is most definitely a must read. This devotional book is so practical and will help enhance your knowledge, wisdom, and understanding about real-life issues and how to embrace each day with the faith you'll need to face whatever decisions, trials, and joys you encounter."

**—Pastor Michael Nelson, Former President**
The National Black Fellowship, Assemblies of God
Pastor of The House of Peace in Jacksonville, FL

"Dr. Darnell Williams has written an amazing book critically examining the life of Joseph, while extracting relevant truths for our lives today. It's a must read!"

**—Bishop Shawn Branham**
Trailblazers Churches

"Too often we rush through the great stories of biblical heroes to their moments of greatness and positions of fame—Moses leading the Israelites through the Red Sea, David ruling on his throne, Daniel using lions' manes as pillows, Esther adorned as a queen seated next to the king, and Joseph in his own regal robes saving not only his dysfunctional family but the nation of Israel. In *Setup for a Breakthrough*, Dr. Darnell Williams takes us on a journey across Joseph's life that begins with promise and betrayal of the worst kind to forgiveness and a generosity of soul forged over years of brokenness and agony where the writer of Genesis keeps inserting into Joseph's story, "the Lord was with Joseph." It is a story with much to say to us today, taking us across Joseph's years from a dream and fancy coat to years of betrayal and false imprisonment and a depth of anguish to a man who held on to the God of his father and whose soul embraced a forgiveness that came at great cost. Joseph's story points to another who offered forgiveness at the greatest cost of all, and we are the recipients of that forgiveness. Thank you, Darnell, for taking us on this journey to discover that the God of Joseph is the same God who extends forgiveness to us and is with us."

**—Dr. Carol Taylor**
Former President of Evangel University

"Dr. Darnell Williams' study takes us back to the timeless truths of Scripture to the life of Joseph and provides a balm for broken and divided hearts. If you have dealt with betrayal or pain in ministry or even in life, I recommend you draw from the healing waters of Scripture through this refreshing resource."

**—Dr. Melissa Alfaro**
AG Non-Resident Executive Presbyter Under 40

# Setup for a Breakthrough—
# The Life of Joseph

Dr. Darnell K. Williams, Sr.

Forward by Darnell Keith Adrian Williams, Jr.

DK Williams Enterprises | Lima, Ohio

Setup for a Breakthrough—The Life of Joseph



DK Williams Enterprises
Lima, Ohio

nexlevelleadership.com

ISBN 13: 9781087977515

*Cataloguing-in-Publication Data*

---

Setup for a Breakthrough—The Life of Joseph by Darnell K. Williams Sr.; foreword by Darnell Keith Adrian Williams, Jr.

xvi + 84 p.; 23 cm. Includes bibliographical references.
ISBN 13: 9781087977515
I. Williams Sr., Darnell K. II. Williams, Jr., Darnell Keith Adrian.
III. Setup for a Breakthrough—The Life of Joseph.

---

Manufactured in the U.S.A.                                                2023



Edited by Lois E. Olena

Cover Design: FIVERR.COM

# Dedication

To my wife—Kim Charlene Williams

My goal in life is to make you the happiest woman on earth!

# Contents

# Foreword

It is my great pleasure to introduce to you the latest work of my dad, entitled *Setup for a Breakthrough—The Life of Joseph*. This book delves into the life of Joseph and reveals how his journey was a long process of God's handiwork in setting him up for greatness—far before he or others in his life could even begin to imagine it. As a lifelong student myself, I have learned (often painfully) the importance of perseverance and patience in the face of challenges.

One of my favorite sayings is, "If failure can't stop you, what can?" This book is a testament to these virtues and to that sentiment specifically, as it highlights the power of staying vigilant and ready in the times of waiting and preparation that we face in our lives.

On a more personal note, my father has always been a man of faith, and his deep understanding of the Word has served as a constant source of inspiration for me. He has a way of bringing the biblical stories to life, weaving in accurate historical contexts, personal insights, and real-life examples that make the lessons he teaches both relevant and applicable to our lives today.

In this book, he takes on the story of Joseph with a skillful and artful touch, unraveling the details of his life in thought-provoking and engaging ways. What struck me most about this book is the way my father illuminates the idea that Joseph's greatness did not come as a sudden burst of brilliance but rather from a long process of preparation in the face of failure, betrayal, and discouragement.

As we journey with Joseph through his trials and tribulations, we see how each step was necessary in shaping him into the man he needed to be to fulfill his destiny. The story of Joseph—and this book—

present a powerful message that speaks to the value of endurance, faith, and trust in the journey and plan God has for each of us.

As the reader, you can expect to be equally inspired, encouraged, and challenged by this book. Whether you are a person of faith or not, the lessons in these pages remain universal and relevant to anyone seeking to live a life of purpose and meaning. I feel confident that my dad's work will leave an indelible mark on your heart and mind, as it has done for me.

I so admire my father, not only for his writing talent but for the man he is—day in and day out. He has always been a role model and example of Godly manliness to me. His dedication to his faith and our family has served as an unwavering source of strength and inspiration. I feel honored to call him my father and to carry his name. I know that his work will continue to impact lives for years to come.

**—Darnell Keith Adrian Williams, Jr.**

# Preface

This book was birthed out of a four-week Bible study that I taught to my congregation. I did a deep dive into Joseph's life. This study will take you on an emotional journey where you will experience Joseph's heart, his feelings, his emotions, and his pains. It was life changing. My prayer is that it can serve as a source of hope and strength to you regardless of your situation.

Remember—

> "Never let your setback be a letdown;
> your setback, just may be a setup
> for your next breakthrough!"

# Acknowledgments

I am grateful for my wife, Kim Charlene Williams. At the time of this writing, we are celebrating thirty years of marriage! Let's go for thirty more!

Likewise, I express gratitude for my son, my namesake, Darnell Keith Adrian Williams, Jr. Son, the Lord has a great plan for your life!

I am grateful for friends! The Lord has placed so many wonderful people in my life.

Finally, I express my gratitude to my Lord! Thank You for calling me into the ministry.

# Introduction

## Joseph's Journey—An Overview

Let's look at the story of Joseph in the Hebrew Scriptures from a different light. Oftentimes we talk about Joseph being a dreamer, Joseph getting his promotion, or Joseph being a person of favor. However, I want to deal with the emotional fallout of the Joseph experience because his story provides biblical context to deal with some real-life issues that Scripture can help us with to live godly.

This book is divided into four chapters. First, we look at Joseph and **betrayal**. We will review how Joseph was ill-treated by his brothers and will consider how the Scriptures indicate to us to respond when we are betrayed. I don't know about you, but I have experienced the bitterness of betrayal, and that is one of the most bitter pills to swallow in life.

Eventually, at some point in your life, you *will* experience betrayal. Someone you have trusted, who you have invited into your life, who you have taken your armor off with (by this I mean, someone you have become vulnerable to, sharing your heart, and showing your scares) is going to see an opportunity to stab you right in the heart. They won't even backstab you; they're going to *front* stab you! They are going to look you right in the eye and betray you. We'll talk about that in Lesson 1.

In Chapter 2, we'll talk about Joseph and Potiphar's wife—looking at the tension of **Joseph operating in favor and being the victim of falsehood.**

What do you do when someone falsely accuses you of something of which, in fact, you are innocent? Oftentimes living in tension of two extremes is the norm for the people of God.

Chapter 3 deals with being **forgotten**. I don't know about you, but I have felt forgotten in life at times—by peers, by friends, by those with whom I'm in relationship. Joseph experienced that pain of being forgotten.

---

Eventually, at some point in your life,
you *will* experience betrayal.

---

The final chapter will look at the power of **forgiveness**. We'll talk about Joseph offering forgiveness to his brothers. When he had the power—and I would argue the right—to avenge his wrong, he decided to practice the God way and forgive. He refused to do wrong to them even though they had done wrong to him.

## Who Was Joseph?

Joseph was one of the Old Testament patriarchs, and as such, one of our great heroes. His story begins with God calling his great grandfather, Abraham. Abraham had a son named Isaac, who had a son named Jacob. Jacob had twelve sons by his wives, Leah, and Rachel, and his two concubines, Bilhah, and Zilpah. Joseph was number eleven. Because Joseph was born to the woman Jacob *really* loved (Rachel), Jacob favored Joseph—treating him as if he was his firstborn.

Joseph was also a great man of faith. The Bible tells us in the Book of Hebrews that Joseph made mention of his bones, saying that he should not be buried in Egypt when he dies, but that they should carry his bones out of Egypt and bury him in the Promised Land. So, the children of Israel took custody of Joseph's bones, and for nearly 500 years kept and honored them. In the Book of Exodus, when God delivered the children of Israel from Egypt, they carried Joseph's bones out of Egypt. Can you imagine such a legacy, that 500 years later, your words, decisions, impact, and lifestyle would affect the lives of your progenitors? What a great man of God!

# A Life Marked by "Ps"

## The Promise

Joseph's life was marked by five words beginning with the letter P. First, we find Joseph with a **promise** over his life. Joseph helps us understand how God sometimes takes us through a process to get the promise fulfilled. If you have ever seen a promise from God, you know it's not a straight line or a linear path. Sometimes you must go through peaks and valleys, climbing over mountain tops and navigating low points. You have your highs and lows, and sometimes it feels tempting to quit during a low point when you feel further away from God's promise than you ever have been. Joseph's story reminds us that we need to trust God.

Joseph was a young man who when he was young received a promise from God that he would be a leader. The mantle of leadership, of being able to administrate and manage people and resources, would come upon his life. This promise came to him when he was about seventeen years old when God visited him and gave him dreams about his life.

Perhaps you have been serving the Lord for a long time, and there were things God spoke to you about even in your youth that you have forgotten about, forsaken, or stopped believing God for. I want to stir up your faith and remind you of the things God has promised concerning your life. May you begin to stir up the promise of God over your life and lay hold to those promises. Regardless of whether you are young and just getting started on your journey or have been on it a little while and have a lot of life to look back on, I want to remind you—we are people of promise!

## The Pit

The next 'P' that marks Joseph's life is that he ends up in a **pit**. Now, how do you serve God and go from a promise to the pit? Well, sometimes that's the way the economy of God works. One of the things you will notice about Joseph's life is that every place along the way, no matter what adversity, obstacle, or external force Joseph runs into, we always find God meeting him right there at the very point of his need. The Lord always promotes Joseph from the back of the line to the front of the line.

You may be like Joseph with a promise, but you feel like you're in the pit. Let me give you hope: the pit is not eternal! God will ensure that you get out of that pit.

## Potiphar's House

The third 'P' in Joseph's life is **Potiphar**. We will talk about who Potiphar was and how Joseph goes in Potiphar's house—rising from his enslavement to run the entire house.

When the blessing of God is on your life, people may try to put you in abject and adverse circumstances. The devil may try to do things to constrict and hinder you, too. But what the devil—and people being used by the devil—don't realize is that your setback is nothing but setup for a breakthrough.

_______________________________________________

Your *setback* is just a *setup*.

_______________________________________________

Listen, your setback is just a setup. As long as you have God in your life—as long as you are serving the Lord—the Lord will never allow the plans of your enemies to prevail. They may prevail for a moment.

They may prevail for a season. It may seem as if you are losing, but with God you will never lose; you will always win. Hallelujah!

Say it: With God, it may look like I'm losing. I might be down. I might look like I got some teeth knocked out. I might be down looking like I'm getting ready to be counted out but *with God, I will never lose; I will always win.* So, my setback is a setup!

## The Prison

Then the fourth 'P' in Joseph's life is that he goes to **prison**. If Joseph were alive today, he would have been registered as a sex offender! He would be labeled a criminal and sent to prison. Yet, even in the prison, God knew him. God found him there and promoted him in the prison.

---

No matter the pressure, the promise is
always going to percolate to the surface.

---

See, no matter the pressure, the promise is always going to percolate to the surface. You may have a mantle of leadership on your life. You've been a leader all your life—on the ballfield, in the classroom, at the school, and on the job. You're just a leader. It seems like no matter where you go, you always get the leader's portion and promoted to the front. That's the blessing of God over your life. Don't get it twisted. It's not by your talent, skill, or ability; it's because God's blessing has sanctified you. The Lord has put His favor on you, and His mantle of leadership is on your life.

## The Palace

The fifth 'P' in Joseph's life is that he finally makes it to the **palace**. God ensures that the *promise* on Joseph's life aligns with the *plans* of his life. God makes sure that the promise always ends up in the palace. We serve the God who Paul declared "can do exceedingly and abundantly above all that you can ask or think" (Eph 3:20), so believe in faith. We serve a God who is bigger than any situation, any circumstance, and any problem. I want to encourage your faith that as you read about the life of Joseph, that you begin to realize that God is working right now in your life.

You may be in the **pit**, metaphorically, or you may be in **prison**. You may feel like you're in **Potiphar's house**, but God is going to make sure that when it's all said and done, the **promise** will be in alignment with the **palace**. God is working, navigating your life so that the promise and the palace always line up together.

## Why Study Joseph's Life?

"For whatever things were written before were written for **our learning** [to educate us with understanding], that **we through the patience and comfort** [to build us up with endurance] of the Scriptures might have **hope** [to encourage us with anticipation]" (Rom 15:4, NKJV).

Why study Joseph? Paul writes in Romans 15:4, "Whatsoever things are written before are written for our learning that we through patience, and comfort of the scripture might have hope" (Rom 15:4). Let's examine this together.

## "Written for Our Learning"

First, Paul says these things that are written are written for our *learning*. They're written to educate us, to give us understanding. They teach us the economy of God and how situations or circumstances work. They give us a realistic outlook on the nature of life, the way it functions. Joseph has a promise on his life but goes through so many obstacles; eventually the promise gets fulfilled, and he goes from the promise to the palace. As the people of God, Joseph's story is written for our learning so we can get knowledge in our heads and understanding in our hearts.

## "That We through Patience ..."

Then Paul writes about patience. The word *patience* in Romans 15:4 means endurance. This is not like the kind of patience I need when I'm patiently waiting for someone (my Uber driver, my door dash, my taxi, my bus, or my flight) or waiting for a phone call. No, it means that *as I am going through life, I learn how to endure.* I develop emotional, physical, mental, psychological, and personal toughness, so that I don't quit. I don't give up. Joseph was presented with an opportunity where he could have quit, but he refused. He endured, and like him, we can endure too.

## "Might Have Hope"

So, Paul writes that Scripture is written for our learning so that we can learn endurance, through which we ultimately can gain *hope.* Hope says, things have to get better. They can't always be like this. It can't always be this bad, this hard, or this difficult.

I heard a powerful quote that says, "People can last forty days without food, three days without water, but they can't last one moment without hope." If you feel hopeless, let me encourage you to hope in God. When David asked the question of himself, "Why are you cast down, O my soul? He responded, "Hope thou in God" (Ps 42:5).

## What are the Lessons
## We Want to Learn?

Joseph remained strong and steadfast. What was the source of his strength? His source of strength was a dream so big that only the Lord could bring it to pass. His life contains many lessons for us to learn from. We do so by looking back over our lives to understand what God is doing and how we are responding.

Søren Kierkegaard said, "Life can only be understood backwards, but it must be lived forwards."[1] My mother used to say, "Hindsight is always 20/20." I guess if she were alive today, she could say, "Hindsight is always HD, 5K, or 8K." In other words, only when we look back over life can we grow to understand what God was doing. I remember when I was a young man, I thought I knew everything about everything. As I have gotten older now, I realize I don't know a whole lot about a whole lot. So, as we approach Joseph's life, we get to see his life backwards, and it gives us understanding. But in *our* life, we're living forward. The reason I want you to have hope is that one day you will look back over your life and see that this season, this moment, this time is fleeting. There will come a day when your present becomes your past, and when you look back on it, you'll be able to see how God was at work. You'll see how the promise of God was not denied just because it was delayed.

So, let's go! Week one we're going to talk about **betrayal**. I will begin with this anonymous quote: "The saddest thing about betrayal is that it never comes from your enemies." Betrayal always comes from someone you know, often someone you trust, someone you invited in, someone you decided to become vulnerable with, someone you befriended, someone you extended out to in order to do life with, someone you have demonstrated trust in and trustworthiness to. You weren't crazy or foolish; that person gave you a reason to trust them—and then betrayed you.

---

[1] Søren Kierkegaard, "Life can only…" Brainy Quote, accessed June 17, 2023, https://www.brainyquote.com/quotes/soren_kierkegaard_105030.

# Chapter 1:

# Joseph and His Brothers (Betrayal)

"The saddest thing about betrayal is that it never comes from your enemies." —Unknown

## Joseph and His Family Dynamics

### Joseph was a Dreamer

"Then they said to one another, 'Look, this dreamer is coming!'"
(Gen 37:19, NKJV).

Understanding Joseph's betrayal involves first grasping the nature of his family dynamics. Genesis 37:19 describes Joseph as a dreamer. Every time a significant shift in Joseph's life occurred, it was punctuated by a dream. The promise of God comes to Joseph because of a dream. Betrayal never comes from your enemy. You know your betrayer, and often you even choose your betrayer. That's what makes it so painful. You *choose* them. You don't choose them to betray you; you've chosen them to befriend you, but they become a betrayer. Joseph the dreamer had dreams and could interpret dreams, so they become a central theme in his life.

### Joseph was Loved by His Father

"Now Israel loved Joseph more than any other of his sons, because he was the son of his old age" (Gen 37:3a, ESV).

Second, Joseph was loved by his father, Jacob, who almost commits a sin by showing favoritism to Joseph. I have three nieces, but when I think back on them as little girls, I would tell all three of them, "You know, you're my favorite." They are grown women now in their thirties and forties, and they still argue who was uncle D's favorite. But I told them all, "You're my favorite."

## Joseph was a Favored Son

"And he [Jacob] made him [Joseph] a robe of many colors" (Gen 37:3b, ESV).

Jacob declared Joseph as his favorite son! Genesis 33:8 says: "Now Israel loved Joseph more than any of his other sons." Joseph was the son of Jacob's old age, and out of all his sons, he showed partiality to Joseph. He showed that sentiment by making for Joseph a coat of many colors. He didn't just give him some decorative outfit. In doing this, he bestowed upon Joseph the birthright of the first born.

We read later of how Jacob meets Joseph and realizes that Joseph has been blessed with two sons, Ephraim and Manasseh. Jacob says to Joseph, in essence, "I'm pushing your inheritance aside, and I'm adopting your two sons as though they are my own. So, I'm taking your one blessing and I'm giving it a double portion." So, he gives Joseph the first-born portion even though he's son number eleven. Joseph's father just favors him. We know Joseph has a younger brother named Benjamin, whose mother dies giving birth to him. Jacob lived with a lot of tragedy in his life.

The family dynamics of the brothers, who are, in fact, much older than him. They're grown men seeing their father extend his favor and love to Joseph, and then they hear this little brother saying he's going to lord over them! I had a little brother; everywhere I went, he wanted to go. Everything I did, he wanted to do. My mother, I guess now looking back, she thought him coming with me would prevent me from doing wrong because my little brother was always with me. In some regards, she was right.

Imagine if your little brother said, "I'm going to be lord over you. I'm going to be your boss one day, you going to work for me, and everything you do is going to pale in comparison to who I will become and what I'm going to accomplish." Man, no one wants to hear that! So that was the kind of relationship and family dynamics going on here. It escalated so much that it created relational fallout.

## Relational Fallouts

## Disunity

"But when his brothers saw that their father loved him more
than all his brothers, they hated him and could not
speak peacefully to him" (Gen 37:4, ESV).

Relational dynamics create fallout first by creating the relational fallout of disunity. Jacob's favoritism and the dream Joseph shared with them caused problems. Sometimes the things God has given you in your heart as dreams are just good *not* to share with anybody. Sometimes it's good to do what the Bible says that Mary, the Lord's mother did. She *thought* on these things, she *pondered* them in her heart. Sometimes it's not good to release your dream prematurely.

Genesis 37:4 says, "but when his brothers saw that their father loved him more than all his brothers," what happened? They hated him; the betrayal that came from Joseph's brothers started with hatred. They hated him and could not speak peacefully to him. Every time they interacted with each other, it was strife, confusion, and anger in the exchanges.

Learn to keep things to yourself. Sometimes if you release them too early, then you invite criticism of your dream. Not everything is meant for you to share with everybody. There are some things God is doing that you just have to let Him mature. When a plant is growing, there's a season called germination. In other words, it's hidden in the dirt. Nobody knows what's going on. You have to let that process play out.

There was disunity; Psalm 133 says, "behold, how good and how pleasant it is for brothers to dwell together in unity." If you do a Bible study on "brothers in the Bible," as my pastor used to say, child, let me tell you, it's a mess! It's a *hot mess*. The first two brothers, one killed the other. And on and on, there seems to be disunity among brothers.

## Discord

"And his brothers said to him, 'Shall you indeed reign over us? Or shall you indeed have dominion over us?' So, they hated him even more for his dreams and for his words" (Gen 37:8, NKJV).

The second aspect of relational fallout was relational discord. Genesis 37:8 says that Joseph's brothers said to him, "Are you indeed going to reign over us? Oh, you think you're going to be the boss over us. Lord over us? Our sheaves are going to bow before your sheaves. The sun, moon, and stars will bow before you? OK, Mr. Big Shot, we'll show *you* how much of a leader and ruler you actually are!" Genesis 37:4 says that they *hated* him because their father loved Joseph. In verse 38, it says they hated him even more for his dreams and his words. So, keep things to yourself. Don't be in the habit of talking a whole lot and oversharing.

## Despising

"Come therefore, let us now kill him and cast him into some pit; and we shall say, 'Some wild beast has devoured him.' We shall see what will become of his dreams!" (Gen 37:20, NKJV).

Third, Joseph's brothers despised their brother. Watch how it escalated. It went from disunity—their hating him because their father loved Joseph—to discord. They hated him now for his dream and for his words. In Genesis 37:20 they say, "Come now let us kill him." These are *brothers*! And you know what's sad, that spirit is still alive in the Church today. That contentious spirit against brothers arises too often, that instead of a person celebrating their brother or sister's dream, they feel they must 'kill' the other person because of the dream. "I don't like him or his words. I don't like her or her words." Don't be small. Be big enough to celebrate when someone else has a dream; be big enough to let someone share with you what God has done for them.

The Bible says in Genesis 37:20, "Let us kill him and throw him into one of the pits. Then we will say a fierce animal has devoured him, then we will see what becomes of his dream." Joseph's brothers thought that by throwing him into a pit they could negate the dream, but the dream wasn't the result of Joseph's own imagination. It was a supernatural download from Almighty God! God had spoken to this young man about his life and about what He was going to do in his life.

They threw him into the pit, took the robe their father had given Joseph, killed an animal, soaked the coat in the animal's blood, and took it to their father. They said, "Is this your son's robe? We don't know if this is it or not. We want you to authenticate." They essentially are saying, "We're not sure it's his. Maybe somebody else had one just like him, but we don't know, could you tell us?" You know what angers me about these young men is when I hear what their father says. He holds the robe of Joseph, and he says, "I will mourn for Joseph for the rest of my life!" Every time I say those words, they are troublesome because you hear this man's broken heart. He already had a wife who had died giving birth to his last son, Benjamin. Now, they come to him saying, "Joseph is dead." He says,

"I'm going to mourn for Joseph the rest of my life. I'm going to go to my grave mourning Joseph. God, how could you take Joseph from me? You could have taken one of the others, not Joseph; not the son in whom I saw so much. God, how could you? So, I'm going to mourn for this boy for the rest of my life." These young men saw their father's broken heart, but they stuck to their devilish, devious, demonic, evil plan.

## Other Biblical Heroes
## Who Faced Betrayal

### Abel

"Cain spoke to Abel his brother. And when they were in the field,
Cain rose up against his brother Abel and
killed him" (Gen 4:8 ESV).

Other biblical heroes faced betrayal. Abel was killed by his brother, Cain, in Genesis 4. Why does he kill his brother? He kills his brother over the fact that he threw his offering together, and God rejected it. Abel was intentional and consecrated his offering to God. Cain was angry that the Lord had rejected his own offering but had accepted his brother's offering.

### King David

"Even my close friend in whom I trusted, who ate my bread,
has lifted his heel against me" (Ps 41:9 ESV).

David says in Psalm 41 that his friend, one like his own brother, had betrayed him. Hear what David says. David faced betrayal, as he articulates in the Psalms. In Psalm 55:12, he says, "It's not my enemy who taunts me. Then I could bear it." He expects his enemy to be his enemy. He says, "It's not an adversary who has dealt so insolently with me. I know how to hide myself from *him*. But you, a man, my brother, my friend, my equal, my companion. We used to take sweet counsel together. You and I had intimate conversation. We used to share together. We break bread together." David even says in Psalm 55, "We walked to God's house together, and you betray me." Betrayal is a bitter pill to swallow, saints. I don't know if you've had to swallow what I have, but it is bitter. It's tough to go down. It gets stuck in your throat. That pill is bitter.

## The Lord Jesus

"Jesus said to him, 'Judas, would you betray the Son
of Man with a kiss?'" (Luke 22:48, ESV).

You know, even the Lord Jesus was betrayed. He asks Judas in Luke 22:48, "Would you betray me with a kiss?" That's how betrayal comes sometimes—with a kiss. As a pastor I have seen people do things that I look back on and refer to as last suppers. It's not really a dinner or a meal, but sometimes when people give you a gift, that's the last thing you hear from them. It happens. I'm sad to say it, but it does happen.

# Results of Betrayal

## Broken Trust

What are the results of betrayal? The first is broken trust. Betrayal creates anxiety, stress, and strain on the relationship. As Joseph sat in that pit, he may have wondered how he could ever trust his brothers again. How could he ever say, "I trust you?" Trust was broken. And when trust gets broken it creates apprehension, distress, and strain in the relationship begin to develop.

## Doubts Develop

A second result of betrayal is that doubts develop. When facing betrayal question of relational identity develops. This relational crisis creates a myriad of questions like, "Who am I? Who are we? What is our future? Help me understand, what does this mean for us moving forward?"

## Remembering and Collecting Offenses

Then you have the aspect of remembering and collecting past offenses. As you reflect on the past, it's easy to take sides and start assessing blame. We say, "I saw this," or "I knew that" and "You caused this or that."

## Hostility

A fourth result of betray is that hostility begins to develop. Hostility expresses itself in one of two ways—fight or flight. The fight response is to become aggressive and combative. The flight response is to become withdrawn or to express a passive aggressive attitude.

## Adjusting

The fifth stage of betrayal is adjustment. There will be necessary relational adjustment. This is the hard part, wrestling with how to move forward? Once betrayal occurs, how do we respond? Here are two pathways forward:

*Positive Outcomes—Improved Role Identity and Restored Relationship*

What we hope for is that the role identity gets addressed and the relationship restored. That's what we strive for. Improved role identity means that we are persevering the relationship, however there are agreed upon and necessary changes that must be made as we move forward.

*Negative Outcomes—Redefined Relationship: Avoidance or Domination*

The second possibility is the negative outcome. This can express itself in two options. The first is relational avoidance—serious damage has been done to the relationship and moving forward together is no longer viable. It is not wise to stay in a relationship where betrayal occurs again and again, where it is never confronted. This is a setup for disappointment, not for a breakthrough.

The relationship must be redefined. In other words, there's either going to be diminished relationship, avoidance, or an increased relationship. If a person has shown themselves to be a toxic, dysfunctional person, then there's no way the relationship is going to be healthy. You cannot have a relationship based on domination.

So only two things will happen when betrayal takes place—either we adjust, and it's going to be positive, or we adjust, and it is going to be negative. If there's a betrayal, it must be one of those two options. It is impossible to maintain the status quo.

## Responding to Betrayal

"In essentials, unity; in non-essentials, liberty;
in all things, charity." —St. Augustine

"Getting to the next level always requires ending something, leaving it behind, and moving on. Growth itself demands that we move on. Without the ability to end things, people stay stuck, never becoming who they are meant to be, never accomplishing all that their talents and abilities should afford them."
—Dr. Henry Cloud, *Necessary Endings*

Let me give you some pointers about responding to betrayal.

### Reflect Biblical Mandates

The first pointer for responding to betrayal is to reflect biblical mandates. Psalm 133 says that dwelling together in unity as brothers is good and pleasant. Ephesians 4:3 urges believers to eagerly maintain the unity of the spirit in the bond of peace. I want to be eager to maintain unity. First Peter 3:8 compels brothers to all have a mind characterized by unity, practicing sympathy with each other. We have a biblical mandate to practice brotherly love and to have a tender heart and humble mind. Hebrews 12:14a says to "Strive for peace with everyone."

To handle betrayal, you must reflect biblical mandates. I was talking to someone recently who said, "Pastor, I feel like killing a family member." I said, "Bro, don't kill him! If you kill him, you are going to go to jail! That's homicide! You can't kill. You just can't do that." And he said, "I know pastor, but I *feel* like it." All of us understand this emotion. Anger, frustration, and pain can push us all toward such feeling. I heard Sam Chand at a conference humorously say recently, "I don't know if you've *really* ever been in the ministry without having the feelings of committing a homicide!" Pain and pressure can bring forth such raw emotions.

## Reject Bitterness

A second response to betrayal is to reject bitterness. When betrayal happens, the devil has an assignment, and that is not just to hurt you, but to spoil your heart. When you experience betrayal, the devil wants to use that betrayal as a gateway, a doorway for bitterness to enter you. Here's what can happen, though. When that bitterness comes in, you can function and fulfill tasks and responsibilities and duty, but your heart is not in it. That's what the devil wants—for you to get bitter behind the betrayal.

---

That's what the devil wants—for you to get
bitter behind the betrayal.

---

Ephesians 4:31 says: "Let all bitterness and wrath and anger and clamor and slander be put away from you." We cannot afford to be bitter. It's too costly. We're going to talk about forgiveness in week four, but I'll say this right now. Someone said, "Unforgiveness is like me wanting to poison you, but I drank the poison instead." That's what happens when you get bitter.

Hebrews 12:15 says, "Let no root of bitterness spring up in you because it makes you defiled." Saints, listen, I've been betrayed. It hurts. Someone reading this may feel the pain; maybe the betrayal just happened, and you're feeling the sting of it. Let me tell you something, work through your bitterness. Work through it because the devil's task is to shut your heart down.

Bitterness gets you to close up. You can tell bitter people; they have a scrawl on their face, a contention in their spirit, a cynicism about them. It may be stuff from twenty, thirty, forty, or fifty years ago. You still talk about it, and the devil is after your heart. Watch out if you close your heart.

---

## Bitterness gets you to close up.

---

I remember when my wife and I went to a pastors conference after we had experienced a bitter betrayal as pastors. Literally, my wife and I wept through an entire box of Kleenex in a forty-five-minute message listening to the main preacher conference in Orlando, Florida. My wife and I just kept pulling clean tissues and wiping our eyes. God used that service as a cathartic moment for us so we could purge those negative emotions out of our spirits.

A profound observation the speaker made concerning betrayal – "The devil's task is to close your heart because of Judas. But once he closes your heart because of Judas, you can't open your heart and receive the love of John." We wept, and we cried. I feel so glad that the Lord delivered us that day from bitterness. Now, we have so many more people with love like John around us than we do with the kind of attitude of that one 'Judas.' We are so grateful for the people of God with us. So don't let the betrayer shut your heart down. Work through the emotion because you must open yourself up.

Not everyone God sends into your life is going to betray you, but watch this on the front end—all lovers look the same. When I say that, I'm not talking about something sexual. I'm talking about brotherly, healthy, relational love. All that love looks the same, but something happens in the heart of the betrayer that changes toward you. It can almost seem like one day all is well, and the next day the world has turned upsidedown. When we experience such a response, we tend to blame ourselves. We look inward, trying to understand this new tension in the relationship. We question our own actions and deeds to see if we have committed some offense that would necessitate such a response. The truth is that you will never understand the motivation of a betrayer. We never quite get a place where their contempt, their issues, and their drama make sense. I am a big believer in emotional intelligence, inward focus, and self-reflection. When it comes to betrayal, though, please understand— no matter how much we look inside, it may never be enough to understand what is happening inside that person betraying you!

## Recognize the Necessary

The third aspect of responding to betrayal is to recognize the necessary. You need to ask yourself three questions: "Do things need to **stay the same**, **change**, or **end**?"

I conclude with an observation by Henry Cloud, who wrote a remarkable book called *Boundaries*. He's a great author and thinker, who merges clinical health with Christian faith. In his book, *Necessary Endings*, Dr. Cloud writes that "getting to the next level always requires ending something, leaving it behind, and moving on. Growth itself demands that we move on. If you're going to grow, there are some things you must leave behind and end."

Many times, your betrayal pushes you into your destiny. Cloud says that without the ability to end things, people stay stuck, never becoming what they were meant to be, never accomplishing all the tasks, sharpening their talents, and maximizing the opportunities afforded to them. You cannot hang onto your past and embrace the future. It's impossible. You must let some things go. Sometimes those things are, in actuality, people you have to leave behind. As a pastor, I have presided over countless funeral services. (In our tradition, we call a funeral a homegoing). Often, I share with the family a quick overview of the grief cycle—anger, denial, bargaining, depression, and acceptance. I love to draw attention to the fact that the last stage is acceptance. Acceptance means that I embrace the reality of the loss and prepare to move forward in life. Notice that the final stage is not resolution! Resolution seeks to understand why something happened. It attempts to give understanding to the mind, trying to answer questions that quite honestly, there is just no answer. So, in moving forward, the call is not to resolution but to acceptance.

---

> You cannot hang onto your past and
> embrace the future.

---

This is why I started out by saying that life is understood looking backward but must be lived forward. Joseph did not understand that this moment in the pit was going to set in motion a series of events that God was setting him up for to get to the palace.

I know your betrayal hurts and is painful, but many times your betrayal comes almost like an evangelist who has preached to you that your seasons are changing, that promotion is on its way, that God is opening a new door and beginning a new chapter. God is doing something new in your life.

Let's revisit Cloud; he says, "Growth itself demands moving on." Ending things is an ability. Ending things is a skill that can be cultivated. People get stuck, and the result of getting stuck is that you never become what you're meant to be because you're trying to carry everything with you from your past into your future.

# Prayer

I want you to be the best you can be for God, for your church, for your pastors, for your brothers and sisters, and for your community. And so, I'm going to pray here for you. If you are dealing with bitterness or betrayal, seeing a 'Judas' right in front of you with a kiss, I know that's painful.

I want to pray for you that you can leave the past behind. The sting of betrayal can create such pain, that forgiveness seems impossible. Let me say to you, it's OK, and it will be OK. Remember, this is a journey. You cannot just take this one teaching as a standalone thing. It's a journey. That's why I call it Joseph's *journey*.

We get to where Joseph gets his promotion, and he says, "Oh, I see now, God was in all of it. And so, what you meant for evil, God meant it for my good." He could have hurt his brothers for hurting him, but he refused. He learned how to let it go, how to move on.

Let me pray for you. Father, in the name of Jesus, I pray for those dear soul who are suffering in silence, for the one whose tears are running down their cheeks, for the one feeling the pain of betrayal, that bitter pill stuck right in their throat, and they are tasting the bitterness like bile.

Holy Spirit, I pray you would come and move and work and manifest yourself. I pray that faith would arise and that we would become hopeful, that we would see the blessing of the Lord come upon us, that we would not be afraid to stand up as people of promise to declare that the Lord is orchestrating our lives and that He has control of us.

Even when our brothers and sisters, those we have invited in, who we have given access to, and to whom we have said, "Come, fellowship with me, worship with me, be a part of my life, let's take a journey together," even when they turn their back on us and betray us, when they lie, tell falsehoods, manipulate the situation, share things they shouldn't share, even with any pain and hurt we feel tonight, Father, I pray in the name of Jesus that you would deliver us and cause healing. We often pray for physical healing, but I pray now for healing of broken hearts. Your Word says you came to bind up the broken hearted. Even when the dish is dropped on the floor and shatters into a thousand pieces, you know how to grab each piece and sweep them back together. Lord God, I pray you would bring those pieces back together and heal each one and bring them to wholeness. Manifest this for your people.

Father, we thank you for Joseph. Thank you for what his life teaches us. We give you praise, in Jesus's name. Amen.

# Chapter 2:

# Joseph and Collision
# (Favor and Falsehood)

"Obviously, I'm not trying to win the approval of people,
but of God. If pleasing people were my goal,
I would not be Christ's servant."
—The Apostle Paul (Gal 1:10)

OK, so in chapter 1 we discussed Betrayal—Joseph being betrayed by his brothers. We talked about the pain linked to betrayal. In this chapter, we will dive deeper into the favor and falsehood that Joseph experienced and the collision of those two realities. Joseph had God's favor on his life, but then he was a victim of falsehood.

Joseph's life was marked by several words beginning with "P." Joseph was a young man full of **promise**. He had dreams. He had visions for his life, and God revealed to him very early on what his ultimate purpose and destiny would be. Responding out of envy, Joseph's brothers threw him in the **pit**. Then they took action and sold him into slavery. He found himself a slave in **Potiphar's** house. He then went from Potiphar's house to **prison**, and from prison, he became prime minister of Egypt in the **palace**. Only God could take someone from prison and turn them into a prime minister. That's the God we serve and the God we will consider in this chapter.

This chapter looks at a challenging and painful part of Joseph's life. The betrayal was one thing, but the falsehood spoken against him was quite another. Here we examine the collision in his life between favor and falsehood. Paul writes to the church in Galatia and says that he is "not trying to win the approval of people, but of God. If pleasing people were my goal, I would not be a servant of Christ" (1:10). We discuss in this lesson about pleasing God and look at how Joseph made a choice totally based upon pleasing the Lord.

## What is Favor?

When you hear the word *favor*, what images come to mind? Perhaps having something bestowed upon you that you didn't earn and don't feel you deserve are the first thoughts that come to mind. You cannot earn favor; God just gives it to you. All you can do with favor is just receive it and say, "Lord, thank you for Your favor on my life."

What does favor look like? Favor looks like people liking you, but they don't know *why* they like you—they just do! It looks like someone going the extra mile for you when they don't have to. Favor looks like when someone opens a door of opportunity for you, and you know you don't deserve the door to be open. Favor looks like when you get to a place or position for which you don't necessarily have the qualifications. Favor is when someone does some type of kindness to you, and they can't even explain to you why they did it. That's the favor of God.

## Joseph was Favored.

### Potiphar's House

"The Lord was with Joseph…" (Gen 39:2).

Joseph had God's favor on his life. Joseph had been thrown in the pit and sold into slavery. In modern day vernacular, we could say that Joseph was a victim of human trafficking. Think about that. He was a victim of human trafficking! He was *sold* and ended up in Egypt.

The man who bought Joseph was Potiphar. Alfred Edersheim, a Jewish historian and scholar who committed his life to Christ, said that Potiphar would have been the head of Pharaoh's *execution squad*, a man who had experienced military success and was probably personally appointed to this position by the Pharaoh, Egypt's king. So, the man who buys Joseph is no man to be toyed with. He's a chief executioner, a direct report to Pharaoh. He purchases Joseph and brings him into his house. Genesis 39:2-6 describes the situation of favor Joseph had in Potiphar's house:

> The LORD was with Joseph, and he was a successful man; and he was in the house of his master the Egyptian. And his master saw that the LORD was with him and that the LORD made all he did to prosper in his hand. So, Joseph found favor in his sight, and served him. Then he made him overseer of his house, and all that he had he put under his authority. So it was, from the time that he had made him overseer of his house and all that he had, that the LORD blessed the Egyptian's house for Joseph's sake; and the blessing of the LORD was on all that he had in the house and in the field. Thus, he left all that he had in Joseph's hand, and he did not know what he had except for the bread which he ate. Now Joseph was handsome in form and appearance (Gen 39:2-6, NKJV).

The fact that the Lord was *with* Joseph is the favor of God. Because the Lord was with Joseph, he was successful. He had been victimized, wronged, and betrayed by his brothers as we discussed in the first lesson. Now he was further victimized by being sold into slavery, yet the Lord was *with* him. No matter your circumstance or situation, always make that declaration. "The Lord is with me!"

Not only was the Lord with Joseph, but he was successful. He was in the house of his master, the Egyptian, and his master saw that the Lord was with him and had made all Joseph's hands did to prosper. So, Joseph found favor in his master's sight and served him. Potiphar made Joseph overseer of his house and put everything under his authority. Also, the Lord blessed this Egyptian's house for Joseph's sake.

When the favor of God is on your life, people will want to connect with you because they see favor over you. They may say, "I want to be connected to you because it looks like everything you do prospers. Everything you do is successful, things move forward, and expand exponentially. You're not a maintainer. You always move things forward!"

---

When the favor of God is on your life,
people will want to connect with you
because they see favor over you.

---

The text goes on to say that the blessing of the Lord was on all Potiphar had in his house and field; thus, he left all he had in Joseph's hand. Potiphar was so confident in Joseph's abilities and believed so deeply in Joseph, trusting him so much, that the only thing he concerned himself with was his bread upon his table.

Can you imagine a boy being purchased as a slave, coming into the home of this man who was an experienced military leader, probably the head of Pharaoh's execution squad, and a direct report to Pharaoh? And he's just saying, "Joseph, you got it, man. You just do what you do." Then the text concludes with these words: "Now Joseph was handsome in form and in appearance." We'll revisit this statement in a moment.

## Favor Plus Diligence Led to Success

"…and he was a successful man…" (Gen 39:2).

There's one thing about favor: favor plus diligence leads to *success*. The Bible says Joseph was a successful man. When you have favor on your life and you put diligence and hard work with it, that leads to success.

## Potiphar Observed That the Lord's Favor was upon Joseph

"…And his master saw that the LORD was with him and that the LORD made all he did to prosper in his hand…" (Gen 39:3).

The aspect of the favor on Joseph's life is that Potiphar *observed* that the Lord's favor was on Joseph. His master saw that the Lord was with him and prospered everything Joseph put in his hands.

## The Marriage of Favor and Diligence Led to Promotion

"…Then he made him overseer of his house, and all that he had he put under his authority…" (Gen 39:4).

This marriage of favor and diligence in Joseph's life led to a promotion. When you have hard work and favor, you will always move up. You'll always go higher. God will always take you from faith to faith, grace to grace, strength to strength, from glory to glory. Favor to favor. That's how it works.

---

Favor without diligence is *presumption.*
Diligence without favor is *fruitlessness.*
Absence of both diligence and
favor is *stagnation.*
The marriage of diligence and favor
results in *success.*

---

Sometimes I hear the saints of God talk about favor. Favor means you must work hard. Favor means sometimes you must get up early to see who's coming in late. Favor means sometimes you sit down and count the inventory after everyone has gone home. Favor sometimes means you keep your head in your books because you have an end goal in mind.

Favor without diligence is **presumption**. When Jesus faced temptation, one of the things He said was, "You shall not put the Lord your God to the test." We don't put God to the test. We ask for favor, but we must be willing to work hard when the favor shows up. Joseph worked; he handled his business.

Diligence—hard work without favor—can sometimes lead to **fruitlessness**. You keep working, working, and working—that's laboring under the curse. What did God say? He told Adam he would work the ground and till it by the sweat of his brow and that because of the curse it would yield thorns and thistles (Gen 3). When you have worked hard without favor, there's fruitlessness, which breeds frustration.

---

When you marry diligence and favor,
God will grant you success.

---

The absence of both diligence and favor is **stagnation**. If you don't have the favor of God and are unwilling to work hard, you're not going anywhere. When you marry diligence and favor, however, God will grant you **success**. Whether you are in ministry or the marketplace, a business owner, or a college student —favor requires diligence, hard work and the result will be success. Think about that.

Favor is bestowed by grace and not something handed out carelessly. Our hard work shows respect for the favor of God. The favored are diligent and highly committed. Favor requires faithfulness and dedication. We can observe favor. We may say, "Oh, I see the favor of God on her or his life," but favor alone is not enough. When Potiphar saw Joseph, the hand of God was on Joseph, and Potiphar observed Joseph's diligence. That's when promotion was extended because Potiphar realized, "This guy's a hard worker. He's committed; he's diligent." So that's why he could extend more favor. Here's a fact about favor—in the economy of God, the more fruitfulness we experience, the more favor grows. And favor brings more favor. Favor attracts more favor. That's why Potiphar could say, "I'm not just going to give you just my checkbook. I'm going to give you *everything* at home—every investment." Can you imagine? "You are going to manage my portfolio, manage my assets, and be the CFO of my industries."

## Joseph and the Falsehood

## Joseph and his *Temptation*

"And it came to pass after these things that his master's wife cast
longing eyes on Joseph, and she said, 'Lie with me.' But he
refused and said to his master's wife, 'Look, my master
does not know what is with me in the house, and he has
committed all that he has to my hand.' There is no one
greater in this house than I, nor has he kept back
anything from me but you, because you are his
wife. How then can I do this great wickedness,
and sin against God?" (Gen 39:7-7, NKJV).

It is remarkable that Pharaoh's chief executioner, a man who had great military success, would have extended trust to Joseph. This is not the type of man who strikes me as being very trusting. This proven warrior and faithful leader charged with the dreadful task of execution was not easily impressed; yet he trusted Joseph. Think about that. He *trusted* Joseph. The Bible says that Potiphar did not even concern himself with anything but the bread that ended up on this table.

In Genesis 39, though, things change for Joseph. His master's wife casts a longing eye on Joseph and says to him, "lie with me," but he refuses. He communicates to her the reality of the trust Potiphar had placed in him, saying that Potiphar has "commanded all that he has" to Joseph's hand. Joseph reminds her, "There is no one greater in this house than I, nor has he kept anything back from me but you, because you are his wife," and then asks, "how can I do this great wickedness and sin against the Lord?"

The Bible says that Joseph was "handsome in form and appearance." This gives some context to the relational dynamic between them. She wanted to have an adulterous relationship with Joseph, but he says, "How can I do this? Your husband has everything under my control. The only thing he's withheld from me is you, his wife." Not only that, but Joseph also calls it a "wickedness" and a "sin against the Lord."

Three lessons exist in this passage with respect to temptation. First, **temptation is *not* sin.** Even Jesus was tempted, as Luke points out: "being tempted for forty days by the devil. And in those days, He ate nothing, and afterward, when they had ended, He was hungry" (4:1-13, NKJV). Jesus was tempted by the devil. If temptation was sin, then the Lord would be guilty of sin, but thankfully temptation is not sin.

Second, **temptation comes in *areas* that tempt us**. As James says, "but each one is tempted when he is drawn away by his own desires and enticed" (Jas 1:14, NKJV). In other words, it's not a temptation if it does not pull on you. If you hate liver and onions, the devil is not going to tempt you with liver and onions; he's going to find the thing that is tempt-able to you, and *that's* the thing he will offer.

Third, **temptation is with us as long as we are in the world**. We live in a sin-cursed world, and as long as we are in this world, temptations will be all around us. We are spiritual people, yet we can still be tempted. As long as we have flesh and blood, as long as our feet walk this earth, we can and will be tempted. If the Lord was tempted, we should not think it strange when we are.

## Christ and Our Temptations

Now, let us take courage and obtain some hope about temptation. First, **Christ aids us in our temptation**. Hebrews 2:18 says: "For … He Himself has suffered, being tempted, He is able to aid those who are tempted" (NKJV).

So, when we are tempted, it's not a time to feel ashamed, run from the Lord, or hide from His presence. It's a time for honesty and a time to ask for help and rely upon His divine aide.

Second, **Christ sympathizes with us in our temptations**. Hebrews 4:15 says, "For we do not have a high priest who cannot sympathize [or we could say it in the affirmative, we *have* a high priest who *can* sympathize] with our weakness, but [who] was in all points tempted as we are, yet without sin" (NKJV). Jesus can sympathize.

The Lord can aid us. He sympathizes with us, and **He makes a way for us when we face temptation**. As 1 Corinthians 10:13 says, "No temptation has overtaken you that is not common to man [humanity]. God is faithful, and he will not let you be tempted beyond your ability, but with the temptation he will also provide the way of escape, that you may be able to endure it."

Every single person gets tempted, but you can bear your cross, surrender your life, and submit to the crucified life. You cannot tell the Lord, "I just lost control. I couldn't control myself. I couldn't take it. I had to give into it." No, the Lord says you won't be tempted beyond what you're able to bear but with the temptation will make a way of escape so you can in fact, endure it.

We all must recognize what areas are our weakest link because that's where the enemy attacks. If we ignore that weakest link, that's where he comes in. We must recognize our area of weakness—whether lying, stealing, being dishonest in some way or cutting corners as opposed to doing things properly, gossiping—whatever that temptation, we all know what it is. We all know where we are easily tempted. Potiphar's wife did not guard herself against her area of weakness. She mused in it. She allowed herself to just immerse herself in it. When the time came and Joseph was there, she gave in. When we think about temptation, we must be honest with ourselves. Admit: "This is a weakness I have. This is an area of struggle for me." You may not tell anyone what it is, but the Lord knows. And I believe *you* know. We must deal with these areas and pray, asking the Lord to really help us overcome our temptation. It's not like a one-and-done thing, either. It's a continuous battle because the enemy comes over and over again.

---

We all must recognize what areas are our
weakest link because that's where
the enemy attacks.

---

The text says that Joseph's master's wife cast longing eyes on him. It was not just that she saw Joseph one time and got infatuated with him. Daily, as Joseph was going through his routines and his responsibilities, executing his role as manager of Potiphar's house, running her husband's home effectively, she is seeing his success, his blessing, and the favor of God. So, she comes to present herself to him.

At the time we live in, we are bombarded with messages of sexual compromise. To so many, there is really no such thing as being "promiscuous" anymore. There is no such thing as "fidelity." It seems like the world is just upsidedown. But Joseph says that to commit this sin would "a great wickedness."

God did not give the Ten Commandments just because He was bored and didn't have anything to do. The Lord knows that if we violate these things, we will have to deal with unintended consequences—shattered lives and broken promises.

The New Testament is replete with warnings concerning sexual purity. Often, David's life is mentioned within this conversation in reference to his sin of adultery. A careful study of the David's life will reveal that his sin against Bathsheba and Uriah set his life on a trajectory of regret. God redeemed David by allowing him to have a son named Solomon who became king, but there were severe consequences for David's sin.

# Joseph's Choice

Sin is a choice. What happens when you yield to temptation? That becomes sin. There's an old hymn that says, "Yield not the temptation, for yielding is sin." When you yield, when you give in to temptation, it is sin. When you give in to your determination to do a thing, that's when you sin.

So first, **Joseph chose moral purity over immoral pleasure**. He made a choice. She said, "Lie with me," but Joseph refused and counteracted her advance. If you look at our culture, if this was played out in a regular context of a "Real Housewives of Egypt," or "The Bachelor of Egypt," Joseph would have gone in and did his thing, and that would have been the end of it. But that's not the man Joseph was and that's not the people God has called us to be.

**Joseph also chose obedience overindulgence**. He says, "you are his wife. What you and my master have is something sacred."

I dare say that probably the system and culture of Egypt, with Joseph as a slave, probably gave Potiphar's wife the right to violate his body in this way. There would not have been a court in the world, in Egypt, that would have upheld Joseph refusing her, but he made the right choice.

---



---

Third, **Joseph chose to honor his favor rather than give way to his flesh**. When favor is on your life, you must handle it carefully. Favor is fragile. He acknowledged that to sin would mean to go against God, the one who had put favor on his life. He responds, "How then can I do this great wickedness, and sin against God?"

## Joseph—the Falsehood and the Fallout

"A lie told against you is like fire. The more you try to
disprove it, the more oxygen you give it.
To put the fire out, starve it of oxygen."
—Dr. Sam Chand

"So it was, when his master heard the words which his wife spoke to
him, saying, 'Your servant did to me after this manner,' that his
anger was aroused. Then Joseph's master took him and put
him into the prison, a place where the king's prisoners were
confined. And he was there in the prison. But the LORD
was with Joseph and showed him mercy, and He gave
him favor in the sight of the keeper of the prison"
(Gen 39:19-21, NKJV).

We have talked about favor and falsehood. Now let's talk further about the fallout. Sam Chand says that "a lie told against you is like fire. The more you try to disprove it, the more oxygen you give it. To put the fire out, starve it of oxygen." Sometimes people lie about you, and there's nothing you can do. I heard an old preacher say, "Ain't nothin' you could do with a lie but outlive it." If you try to chase down a lie, all you're doing is giving it more life. Just outlive it!

So, Joseph literally runs from Potiphar's wife and leaves his robe behind. She wickedly takes his robe, goes to her husband, and says, "Your servant did to me after this manner." The Bible is being very kind there. Let's just talk about what was really going on. She is saying, "That slave you brought in this house raped me."

How can you have the favor of God on your life and have someone lie about you like that? Sometimes the lie testifies of the favor. The lie comes *because* the favor is there. The text says that Potiphar's anger was aroused. Can you imagine the scene? Very imaginative. I could imagine Potiphar grabbing Joseph by his collar, dragging him through the streets, taking him to prison, and locking him up. In verses 19-21, it says Joseph's *master* took him to the prison. Now, if Joseph had been purchased by anyone else, he would have ended up in just a regular 'county jail.' Potiphar, though, was Pharaoh's executioner and direct report; he had access to the king's prison.

## Joseph—Prison and Divine Providence

"Never let your setback be a let down! Your setback just may
be a setup for your next breakthrough." —DKW

So, Potiphar confines Joseph to prison. Hear what the text says:

> But *the LORD was with Joseph* and showed him mercy, and He *gave him favor in the sight of the keeper of the prison.* And the keeper of the prison committed to Joseph's hand all the prisoners who were in the prison; whatever they did there, it was his doing. The keeper of the prison did not look into anything that was under Joseph's authority, *because the LORD was with him; and whatever he did, the LORD made it prosper* (Gen 39:21-23, NKJV).

The Lord was *with* Joseph, showed him *mercy*, and gave him *favor* in the sight of the keeper of the prison. This young man had the favor of God. No matter where he went, you couldn't stop God's favor on his life. Even after Joseph is **victimized**, **ill-treated**, and **wrongfully accused**, he still has the favor of God on his life. He was sent to the prison and put into the prison—but not just any prison. Divine Providence was at work. He was put into the prison where the king's prisoners are confined.

- Joseph was victimized – "Your servant did to me after this manner."

- Joseph was ill-treated – "[H]is [Potiphar's] anger was aroused."

- Joseph was wrongfully accused – "Then Joseph's master took him and put him into the prison."

By way of the falsehood against Potiphar (committed by his wife), Joseph gets imprisoned in Pharaoh's personal prison. You know how this story goes. You know the Bible. In modern-day language we would say: Joseph, a victim of human trafficking, becomes a convicted felon and registered sex offender, but the Lord was with him. The Lord favored him.

---

No matter where Joseph went, no one could stop the favor of God on his life.

---

Psalm 105 describes Joseph's prison experience: "He sent a man before them—Joseph, who was sold as a slave. They hurt his feet with fetters, He was laid in irons. Until the time that his word came to pass, the word of the LORD tested him" (Ps 105:17-19, NKJV).

I find Psalm 105:17 interesting. It says: "The Lord sent a man before them, Joseph." Before whom? The tribes of Israel. They were then just in one big family, but God sent Joseph, sold as a slave, before them. It says they [the Egyptians] hurt his feet with fetters and lay irons on him. Until the time God's word came to pass, the word of the Lord tested Joseph. Dragged into jail, locked away, thinking his time was over, his opportunity lost, his dreams about to die because he's in prison—Joseph does not know that God was strategically ordering every step he was taking.

God does not waste experiences. He always has a plan. Sometimes it's difficult for us to decipher that plan amid the confusion. I can imagine how difficult it was for this young man as he was going through all this. So where was God in all this? He may have asked, "Why do I have to experience this?" But all along, Jehovah God had a plan. He was working on, testing, and trying that plan because He knew Joseph had to be the forerunner of His people. Joseph had to be the one God was going to put out front to lead His people out of Egypt one day.

---

Joseph had to be the one God was going
to put out front to lead His people
out of Egypt one day.

---

Sometimes in our lives as we experience hardship and are on the Potter's wheel, it's hard. The Potter is pressing, pushing, and molding. Sometimes the Potter has to break us up again and start over. It's hard. Sometimes that's the time you want to jump off the wheel and run, give up, give in, and question where God is. But God is right in the midst of everything working because He is a strategic God, a God of a plan. He's not just a God of spontaneity; He always has a plan.

Joseph understood that favor was on him. He understood his responsibility and his commitment. That's why when Potiphar's wife went to him, he could lay out the reality of the situation in almost step-by-step detail. "This man trusts me. He gave me everything, control over his home." Joseph understood his place. He understood that he didn't accomplish all he had because of his good looks or education. He understood that if it was not for God, Potiphar would not have trusted him.

Sometimes as we give ourselves to the things of God, we realize that only the grace of God put us in places and moved us around. That recognition makes us honor our responsibility. It may entail something as simple as sweeping the church, but we can give ourselves to it wholeheartedly. We recognize that the favor of God has granted us this place, that He is working all the time, and that His work will be accomplished.

Joseph had made up his mind ahead of time. He had settled his value system ahead of time. He knew he was a young man in a strange land and time with strange people. But he was determined. "Here are my values, and I'm not going to compromise them, come what may." Have we done that? Do we follow Joseph's model? Because sometimes when the temptation presents itself, if we haven't settled on our values, it's easy to give in to it.

We must decide we are not going to negotiate. There are just some things that, just like now we have a national *do not call* list, that we need to have a *do not do* list. We can decide, "This is something I just won't do."

"So, the Lord was with Joseph and showed him mercy. He gave him favor in the sight of the keeper of the prison." Here we go—wash, rinse, wash, and repeat. Same story over again. Just as Joseph had favor in Potiphar's house, now the favor of God shows up for him in prison. The keeper of the prison committed to Joseph's hand all the prisoners who were in the prison, so whatever they did, it was his doing. The keeper of the prison did not look to anything that was under Joseph's authority because the Lord was with him, whatever he did, and the Lord made him prosper." The blessing of God showed up on Joseph even in prison.

Sometimes God has to take us through
hard places, difficult seasons, and tough
times to accomplish His plan for our lives.

I have a good friend, Dr. Sam Huddleston. He says, "I don't know how you brothers pastor who haven't been in the penitentiary. All the lessons I needed to survive the ministry, I learned in the penitentiary." Nobody wants to go to prison. Nobody wants to go into a pit. Nobody wants to be in Potiphar's house. But sometimes God has to take us through hard places, difficult seasons, and tough times to accomplish His plan for our lives.

Never let your setback be a letdown. Your setback just may be a setup for your breakthrough. When you're set back, when it seems like you are moving in the wrong direction, remember: Joseph could have felt that way—"I'm now further from my promise, here in this in prison. How am I going to be a ruler or leader when I'm in prison? God, was it your plan for me to lead in prison? *That* was your plan, in *prison*?" Never let your setback be a letdown. Your setback just may be a setup for your next breakthrough. That's what God did for Joseph.

Never let your setback be a letdown.
Your setback just may be a setup
for your breakthrough.

Sometimes it looks like what God is doing doesn't make sense when you're going through tough situations. We can look back at Joseph's story and see the hand of God all through the process. If you would have asked Joseph, though, he may have been like, "I'm just being faithful. I don't know what's going to happen. I don't know if I'm going to get out of here." Sometimes it's just us trusting in God and saying, "God, I believe you have my best interests at heart."

Remember Romans 15:4? That's how we started. These things are for our learning, for our understanding, that we might gain endurance. Joseph's story is there to give you endurance. Things may not make sense, but you have the wherewithal, the ability, and the internal fortitude not to quit.

God is going to give you hope. I believe Joseph lived with a hope to say, "God, this is not the way you're going to let this end. This cannot be the way my life is going to work out. This cannot be." And it *wasn't* the end. In the next chapter, we see that Joseph talks to the Butler in prison and says, "Remember me. Tell Pharoah about me. Tell him I'm here, that I was in prison unjustly, that these things have befallen me. Tell him. Maybe God will use you to get to turn my situation around."

---

The Lord is giving you a second chance.
He's going to reset things for you. He's
going to allow you to be a different person.

---

I know you might feel like Joseph, asking, "God, where are you? Did you forget me, Lord? Why does it seem like I'm going further and further away from the very word you spoke to me? This is not some conjuring up of my own imagination. You revealed your will to me."

I'm going to pray that God will give you the strength and endurance to keep running, the aggression to keep fighting, the courage to keep moving. Maybe you've been compromised. Maybe you've been saying, "Well, God has been so gracious and gives so much, but I've been dishonoring His favor on God my life." Maybe you've been saying *yes* when you should say *no*. Or you've been saying *no* where you should say *yes*. The Lord is giving you a second chance. He's going to reset things for you. He's going to allow you to be a different person.

# Prayer

Father, in the name of Jesus, I pray for your people, for those hurting, frustrated, who feel like giving up, who say, "I don't know if it's even worth me taking the next step." Father, I pray in Jesus's name that strength will be upon your people, that fear, anxiety, stress, and worry will not be their portion.

Holy Spirit, I invite the anointing and the power of your Spirit to come. You know whose heart is heavy. Your Word says that when our hearts are overwhelmed, we can ask you to lead us to the rock that is higher than we are. You are higher, deeper, stronger. So, I tap into that strength. Your Word says, "Let the weak say I am strong," so I declare the strength of the Lord over people in Jesus's name. I pray that each person reading this would have the internal fortitude to be a person of high moral caliber.

Lord, I pray right now for every backslider, each one wandering in the fields of the world, indulging in things they know they have no business getting involved in. Father, I pray you would let forgiveness reign. Embrace those returning to the Father's house in Jesus's name.

Father, I thank you for the anointing and for the power of your Spirit. I thank you for the authority of your Word. I thank you for your presence. You promise never to leave us nor forsake us. Thank you, Lord, that you have given us the victory that overcomes the world, even our faith. I thank you in the mighty name of Jesus, and I give you praise, honor, and glory in Jesus's name. Amen.

# Chapter 3:

# Joseph and the Baker (Forgotten)

""The worst happened, and then it passed. You lost the person you thought you couldn't live without and then you kept living. You lost your job then found another one. You began to realize that "safety" isn't in certainty—but in faith that you can simply keep going."

— Brianna Wiest

On Joseph's journey, we find him in prison, unjustly accused of a horrific crime of which he is innocent. His brothers selling him into slavery set in motion a series of events. They thought they were doing evil to their brother, not knowing that God was doing him good behind the scenes.

So often we curse the pain, curse the night, and curse the darkness. Let me tell you, God does some of His greatest work in the midst of pain. God does some of His greatest work at midnight. God does some of His greatest work when all hope is lost. My family endured a painful situation recently. My son was admitted to the hospital in renal failure. My wife and I walked into his hospital room and heard the doctors wrestling with the reality that a healthy twenty-year-old's kidney had just stopped. As you can imagine, it was a low point for my family; it was midnight. This was one of the darkest moments for us. I will never forget the feeling of utter powerlessness we felt. We prayed! We invited the saints to pray! Twelve days later, he was discharged with restored kidney function.

## The Setup – The Butler and the Baker

"It came to pass after these things that the butler and the baker
of the king of Egypt offended their lord, the king of Egypt.
And Pharaoh was angry with his two officers, the chief
butler and the chief baker. So, he put them in custody
in the house of the captain of the guard, in the prison,
the place where Joseph was confined" (Gen 40:1-3, NKJV).

We're going to talk about the setup. God had set Joseph up. He got
sent to jail, where he met the butler and the baker of the Pharaoh
(King of Egypt) who had offended him. He got angry with them, so
he put them in custody, in the house of the captain of the guard—
in the prison where Joseph was also confined.

---

God does some of His greatest work
in the midst of pain.

---

These two fellows had done something—the Bible does not say
what exactly—that got Pharaoh upset with them. They just didn't go
into any prison; they went where officials who have wronged the
state and Potiphar (being Pharaoh's executioner) had access to this
prison. When Joseph had offended Potiphar, he threw him into this
same prison.

## The Heart of Joseph

"And Joseph came into them in the morning and looked at them
and saw that they were sad. So, he asked Pharaoh's officers
who were with him in the custody of his lord's house, saying,
'Why do you look so sad today?' And they said to him,
'We each have had a dream, and there is no interpreter
of it.' So, Joseph said to them, 'Do not interpretations
belong to God? Tell them to me, please'" (Gen 40:6-8).

Three important points arise here. First, **Joseph did not allow the trials on his journey to cause him to become bitter**. I often try to interject myself into biblical stories. I imagine me being Joseph, being betrayed by brothers, being lied to, and thrown into prison. I wouldn't want to have anything to do with anybody. Let's just be honest. I wouldn't want to talk to anyone. I would have isolated myself. Matter of fact, I probably would have done something to get into isolation so I could be by myself. Joseph, though, goes and says, "I can tell something is not right with you guys. What's going on? Talk to me, tell me." He did not allow the trial to make him bitter.

Second, **Joseph found the strength to be a caring person rather than becoming self-absorbed**. There is something about adversity that if you're not careful, you can just create a narrative around you; all you do is walk around with a mirror up in front of you. You always talk about what *you* need and what *you* want, what *you* desire and what's not right for *you*, and how *this* happened and *that* went on, and *this* went down, and such-and-such a person treated you *that* way. Joseph didn't walk around with a mirror, though; he walked around with a window—glass that allowed him to look out from his own situation and see others, not self-reflective glass where he just became absorbed and caught up in himself. He showed concern for others and was a caring person, as opposed to becoming self-absorbed.

Third, **Joseph practiced resilience—the capacity to recover quickly from difficulty**. You know, I like sports. I watch my fair share. I'm not a big basketball fan. I like football more because I understand it more. I played it when I was a little boy and did some coaching of it in Peewee football when my son was playing. So, I know football better, but I enjoy watching basketball. And I was shocked to hear that LeBron James, probably the greatest player alive today, spends a million dollars per year on a resilience program. He has trainers, massage therapists, cryo-treatment, dieticians, and nutritionists—all who help his body recover. Because when he plays, he goes full-bore. He gives 100% and needs to help his body repair and recover quickly.

Pastor, author, and broadcaster, Bob Gass, notes the following traits of resilient people:

1. They take *control* of their lives.

2. They surround themselves with the *right people*.

3. They allow their pain to spur *growth* instead of collapsing in *self-pity*.

4. They insist on changing what they can and *not worry* about the rest.[1]

That's what resiliency is. When you are under immense stress and pressure, you need to have robust strength in your spirit that helps you rebound after the difficulty.

If you're going to be a person who recovers quickly from adversity, this does not mean you will not *face* it, that's not what I'm talking about. Rather, when you *do* face difficulty, here's how to be resilient. First, Gass says, **resilient people take control of their lives**.[2] They take control. If you're going to be resilient, if you are going to bounce back quickly, if you're going to recover quickly, you must take control. You can't let things shipwreck you. You can't let things cause your demise. You cannot act as though there is no God. You must take control of the situation by being mature doing what's right even when you may not feel like it.

---

[1] Bob Gass, "Resilient People," Converging Zone, accessed September 28, 2023, http://www.convergingzone.com/ricciardelli/resilient-people-by bob-gass/, as quoted in Samuel R. Chand, *Leadership Pain: The Classroom for Growth* (Nashville: Thomas Nelson, 2015), 194-195.

[2] Ibid.

Second, Gass says that **resilient people surround themselves with the right people**.[3] When we were kids and another kid would pick on you, somebody else might say, "You don't have to take that, man! You don't have to put up with that!" Because they wanted to see a fight. But that's the wrong type of people to be around. The right people can be honest and transparent with you. They practice candor with you. They tell you the truth, even when you don't want to hear it.

All of us need people. I have people in my life who are unimpressed with titles and positions. You need people in your life who are not impressed with all that stuff, who can just say, "Bro, I see this going on in you; talk to me about it. Tell me what's going on." Joseph saw that in prison and asked the butler and the baker what was going on. You need the right people in your life if you're going to be resilient.

Now, if you want to just respond carnally and in a worldly way and do things that are ungodly and against Christ and that violate the Scriptures, then *anybody* can help you with that. But when you have the right people, godly people who love you, then they want God's best for you and can tell you the truth.

Sometimes it's painful to hear what honest people have to say. I have a friend who's going through hell with his family right now. We have someone who's like a mutual father to us. We were sitting and talking with this man who is like a father to us, and he just laid into my friend. I mean, I was feeling sorry for the brother. He just said, "You need to stand up. You don't sit down and take this. You need to do this, and you need to do that." And it was painful, but you know

---

[3] Ibid.

what? He said, "Brother, I needed that. I needed somebody to tell me the truth." So resilient people have the right people around them.

Third, **resilient people allow their pain to spur growth instead of collapsing into self-pity**.[4] I've talked a lot about that, so I'm not going to elaborate on it. Don't walk around with a mirror. Walk around with a window that you can *look out of* rather than a mirror that you use to keep looking inward.

Your pain should cause you to grow. You are going to find this with Joseph as we get to the end of this lesson, and as we talk about next week, how Joseph instead of when he had the power to command that his brothers be killed breaks down and cries, rather than killing them. He cries on their shoulders and says to them, "I am your brother, Joseph. The one that you sold with all those years ago."

Don't waste a painful lesson by remaining the same person. That lesson cost you heartache, heartbreak, tears, anxiety, stress, and worry. You must pray through it—wrestle with the word *through*—and then get on another side of it. Would you just let that be wasted? No! Let that pain help you grow. If you want to read more about this, one of my heroes who's written a great book called *Leadership Pain* is Dr. Sam Chand. As a matter of fact, I got this Bob Gass quote from *Leadership Pain*.

---

Your pain should cause you to grow.

---

Fourth, Gass says **those who are resilient can recover quickly from difficulty**.[5] He says they insist on changing what they can do and don't worry about the rest. Isn't that insightful? Because oftentimes we worry so much about things we cannot change. Don't

---

[4] Ibid.
[5] Ibid.

worry about what you cannot change. Focus on what you can change and put your efforts and energy around that. Many times, when you're going through these difficulties, the only thing you can change is yourself. When it is rainy, you can't stop the thunder and the lightning. You can't stop the rain from falling, but you can change your behavior. You can learn that you need to pack an umbrella. You can learn how to pull it out, and you can learn how to create a coping system that helps you survive the rain and the storms.

## Joseph Interprets the Butler's Dream

"Now within three days Pharaoh will lift up your head and
restore you to your place, and you will put Pharaoh's cup
in his hand according to the former manner, when you
were his butler" (Gen 40:9-13, NKJV).

So, Joseph says to the butler, "Tell me your dream." Joseph practices resilience. He hears the dream and then tells the butler that Pharaoh will lift up his head and restore him to his place. He's talking to the butler. He says that the butler will put Pharaoh's cup back in his hand as he did formerly when he was the butler.

The baker, though, didn't have as good an outlook as the butler did. Joseph tells him, "Yeah, you're not going to make it back. Potiphar's waiting on you. You have a date with the executioner." The butler got a better report—Pharaoh would restore him.

Watch this, **when God's mantle of leadership is on your life, you will often be in a place where you have to muster the inner strength to minister to others *while* enduring your personal test and trial.** The pain of Joseph's circumstance did not just lift from him. No, *while* he was in it, he ministered. See, when the mantle of leadership is on your life, you will be called many times to minister— even while you've got your own pain. As a pastor, many times I wished someone would pray for me while I was praying for others.

I wish someone would have prophesied to me when I was prophesying to others. I wish someone would have preached to me when I was preaching to others. Oftentimes when you have that mantle of leadership, you have to minister to someone else while dealing with your own pain.

That's why we train our elders, deacons, ministers, and people who work at the altars. Why? Because people must know how to almost pause their pain to be able to create space so God can speak.

Even Jesus ministered to others amid His own pain. In Luke 23:42-43, we find Jesus on the Cross. Talk about dealing with pain! Death had shrouded our Lord like a python and was crushing the life out of Him, but the man—a thief—next to him says, "Lord, remember me when you come into your kingdom." And Jesus says, "Today you will be with me in paradise." And then Jesus dies. That's a picture of ministry! Sometimes you have to pause your own pain to minister to somebody else. Your pain is never an excuse not to have the capacity to minister to someone else.

## Joseph's Hope

"But remember me when it is well with you, and please show kindness to me; make mention of me to Pharaoh and get me out of this house. For indeed I was stolen away from the land of the Hebrews; and also, I have done nothing here that they should put me into the dungeon" (Gen 40:14-15 NKJV).

1. **Remember Me** – Hebrew – "Reflect upon the good I did for you."

2. **Show Kindness to Me** – "Do kindness." – Show Lovingkindness and Be Faithful

3. **Mention Me** – "Call to mind memories of me."

4.   **Get Me Out** – "Create a point of exit."

So, Joseph gives the butler a prophetic word: "Listen, you are going to get restored." And then hear what he says in vv. 14-15, "But remember me." Joseph thinks, *I see now, God, maybe this is what you've been up to all along off. You got me here so this butler can go back to Pharaoh and tell him about me.* He says, "Remember me when it goes well with you. When Pharaoh restores you, please show kindness to me and make mention of me to Pharaoh and get me out of this place. He says, remember me. The Hebrew says, reflect on the goodness that I've shown you. Remember me. He says, be kind to me, show kindness to me. Joseph's life didn't have much kindness to it. His brothers were cruel to him, betrayed him. Potiphar wasn't kind to Joseph. It was a highly transactional relationship. Potiphar's wife caused Joseph to be in prison. Joseph was not accustomed to kindness except from his father Jacob. Joseph was maybe about twenty-eight years old at this stage of his life, being sold into slavery at seventeen or eighteen and now after ten years, all he's experienced is hurt, pain, rejection oppression.

---

We've seen the blessing of God show up,
but that doesn't mean
Joseph didn't carry pain.

---

Now we've seen the blessing of God show up, but that doesn't mean Joseph didn't carry pain. So, he says, "Please, be kind to me. Show empathy, show some compassion on me. Remember me, make mention of me, call me back to your memory and get me out of here. I have got to get out of here." All Joseph is thinking is, *Get Pharaoh to give me a pardon so I can get out of prison. If I just get out of prison, I'll be happy. I'll go on with my life. I'm going to leave Egypt. You won't have to worry about me anymore. I'll get back to living,* but God had another plan.

# The Baker's Dream –
# Doomed to be Executed

## Joseph Forgotten – (v. 43)

"Yet the chief butler did not remember Joseph,
but forgot him" (Gen 40:23, NKJV).

"We have two choices: We can become disillusioned and embittered,
or we can use that difficulty as a platform for putting our hope and
trust in the living God." —Chuck Swindoll

Genesis 40:16-22 tells the story about the baker, how he's going to be executed and then in verse 43, I think these are some of the most painful words in the Bible, "Yet the chief butler did not remember Joseph, but forgot him." Being forgotten is painful.

Chuck Swindoll in his biography of Joseph, when talking about this period in Joseph's life, says we have two choices. We can become disillusioned and embittered, or we can use that difficulty as a platform for putting our hope and our trust in a living God.

*Being Forgotten is Painful!*

Joseph was forgotten. I don't know about you, but I have felt the stinging pain of being forgotten. So, I want to talk here about how to deal with it when you feel forgotten. Being forgotten **makes us question our value**. When someone forgets you, you say, "Do I really matter to you? Do I really have a value in your life? How could you forget me?" Joseph gives the butler this powerful, prophetic word of hope, and you would think the first thing he would do when he went back to Pharaoh was to say, "Let me tell you about this guy I met in prison." Nope. He gets restored and totally forgets.

Second, **being forgotten can create self-doubt**. When others forget you, you could be tempted to say, "Maybe I just need to neglect myself. Maybe because I'm not worth their time, maybe because I'm not valued, maybe I need to just…, what difference do I even make?" You start to embrace self-doubt. You doubt your competency, your abilities, and the call of God on your life.

---

We can use difficulty as a platform for
putting our hope and trust
in a living God.

---

Third, **being forgotten can cause disillusionment**. You lose your hope and lose your way. You just think, *what difference does it make? Why am I trying so hard, just to be forgotten?*

*Being Forgotten is Keenly Felt*

Being forgotten can be keenly felt. Here is when being forgotten can be felt: in times of **testing, trial, and tribulation** going on in life. When you are forgotten in such moments, you feel it.

The second time you keenly feel forgotten is in times of **transition, when you are moving from one season to the next season** of life, being forgotten is keenly felt when it seems like people who were in your life for one season depart as you approach another season. And you're thinking, *I thought we were in this together, I thought we were taking a journey together. I thought you and I were going to be about our Father's business together*, but no, they depart. Sometimes that's a part of change in seasons of transition, being forgotten, you know.

Being forgotten also is keenly felt when we are in a time of **transformation, a time of dying and rebirth**. When the Lord calls us into a season of dying, there's always a season of rebirth. Calvary's never the end. There is always a beginning because there's a resurrection coming. There's a day of renewal, refreshing, rebooting, remaking.

# Promises When We Feel Forgotten

When we feel forgotten, it is important to hold on to some core, true promises from the Lord.

- **The Lord is Protecting Us** – "For thus says the LORD of hosts: 'He sent Me after glory, to the nations which plunder you; for he who touches you touches the apple of His eye'" (Zech. 2:8, NKJV).

Number one, **remember that the Lord is always protecting you**. Listen, I know that when you feel forgotten, sometimes it makes you feel as though you're not valued, but God says you're the apple of His eye! That means you have a special place in His sight—a unique position of favor toward Him. He is watching over you and protecting you. Even when the nations come to plunder against you, as Zechariah says, the Lord says, "I got you." Hear the word of the Lord; He says you are the apple of His eye. No test, no trial, no one turning their back on you is going to make the Lord reject you.

- **The Lord Values You** – "'Your words have been harsh against Me,' Says the LORD, yet you say, 'What have we spoken against You?' You have said, 'It is useless to serve God; What profit is it that we have kept His ordinance, and that we have walked as mourners before the LORD of hosts? So now we call the proud blessed, for those who do wickedness are raised up; They even tempt God and go free.' Then those who feared the LORD spoke to one another, and They shall be Mine,' says the LORD of hosts, 'On the day that I make the LORD listened and heard them; So, a book of remembrance was written before Him For those who fear the LORD And who meditate on His name.' On the day that I make them My jewels. And I will spare them as a man spares his own son who serves him" (Mal 3:13-18, NKJV).

The second promise is that **the Lord values you**. In Malachi 3 the prophet asks questions, and these questions are God repeating back to the people what he's been overhearing them say about Him. The Lord says, I've been overhearing your conversations; you've been saying things like it's useless to serve the Lord. What profit is it if we keep His ordinances and that we have walked as mourners before the Lord of hosts?

The Lord has a promise for when you feel forgotten. There are those getting frustrated with serving God, but there is another cohort sincerely serving the Lord. And the Lord says, "I've been overhearing not only what my critics have been saying, I've been overhearing what my praisers have been saying." He says He has written a book of remembrance—has written the words of the praisers down (those who fear the Lord and meditate on His name). God says He will make those praisers His *jewels* and will spare them as a man spares his own son who faithfully serves him.

God hears what you say. You are not forgotten. You have value. Dear child of God doesn't feel that the Lord has departed from you. No, He loves you. He honors you. He treasures you. He's written down your praise. Can you imagine? God is standing there, like in the shadows, almost like eavesdropping on what you've been saying. You've been talking about how good and faithful He is. In the midst of your test, listen, He has written it down and made a record of your words of praise and faithfulness! So, if you've been forgotten, know the Lord values you. He's protecting you. He values you.

- **The Lord Knows Everything About Us** – "You know my sitting down and my rising up; You understand my thought afar off" (Ps 139:2, NKJV).

Third, **the Lord knows everything about us**. When you feel like you're forgotten, you need to remember that the Lord knows everything about you. Psalm 39:2 says, "You know my sitting down and my rising up, you understand my thoughts when they're still far off." The Lord Jesus told His disciples, "The very hairs of your head are numbered; if a little bird falls from the sky, God takes note of it." Then He says, "How much more does He know and care about you?" The Lord knows everything about you. Listen, the Lord knows your season of life. He knows your time. He knows what you need. He knows the concern on your heart. He knows what's keeping you up at night. He knows what's making you weep. He knows what's making you cry. He knows when you feel challenged. He knows when you feel frustrated. He knows who's causing you pain right now in your life. The Lord has not forgotten you.

People may forget you. Sometimes they do it on purpose. Sometimes it's just a result of faulty human faculties. A brother walked up to me this week and said, "Pastor Darnell, do you remember meeting me? You remember you took me to your church, and we had a conversation with so-and-so and…" then he named the people. So, I know he's not lying to me, and I consider myself a people person. I can remember faces. I remember names. I know how to associate them with places, but I have never seen this guy before in my life. However, he's standing right there telling me how he spent an afternoon with me. Sometimes our forgetting is just the result of human frailty. It's not that people willfully mean to forget, they just do. But watch this: the Lord knows *everything* about us. He values us and is protecting us.

- **The Lord will Never Forget Us** – "Can a woman forget her nursing child, and not have compassion on the son of her womb? Surely, they may forget, Yet I will not forget you" (Isa 49:15, NKJV).

Fourth, **the Lord will never forget you**. In this Isaiah 49 passage, God asks His people a very odd question about the woman forgetting her nursing child. Think about that. You know, the Bible Malachi concludes by telling us that the hearts of the fathers should be turned back to the children and the hearts of the children turned back to their fathers. You know, on Mother's Day, you get flowers and dinners and everything—and Father's Day can almost come and go! There's something about being a mother. I mean, this woman conceives this child, it grows in her womb, and occupies space within her body. She gives birth to this child, holds that child up to her breasts and lets that child nurse. Then she puts it in the crib and forgets she has this child? That to me is almost impossible! I don't think there's ever a woman who would do that, unless there was some mental health issue going on, who would just forget that she gave birth to a child. The Lord says, though, that He will *never* forget you.

## A Word for You

The Lord says that the woman who forgets her child does not have compassion on the child of her womb. He says, "Surely, she may forget, as impossible as that seems, but even if it happens," the Lord says, "I will not forget you." It's impossible for God to forget about us. He is ordering our steps. He knows the plans He has for us.

He says to you: I'm going ahead of you and making every crooked pathway straight. I'm bringing down every mountain. I'm raising up every valley. I'm making every rough place smooth. I'm going ahead into your future so that when you get there, there's a place prepared specifically for you. I will never forget you.

There's a song that says, "I'm not forgotten, He knows my name." The Bible says that Joseph stayed in prison *another two years*. Then finally, God gives Pharaoh a dream, and it's so disturbing to him that he can't sleep. He calls in all his officers and says, "I had this dream, and I need somebody to tell me what it means." And the butler is like, "Oh, you remember that time you got upset with me and threw me in prison—the baker and me—and he got killed, but I got restored? Well, while I was there this little Hebrew boy I met interpreted dreams for me, and everything he said came to pass. Maybe he could help you." And Pharaoh says, "Send for him right now."

Joseph didn't know that night when he went to bed that when he got summoned from that prison, that he would *never* go back to it *ever* again. He went from the prison to becoming prime minister, running Egypt. That's the God that we serve.

## Prayer

God hasn't forgotten you. I want to pray for you, to prophetically declare over your life that we serve El Shaddai, The Almighty God, the God who has more than enough. He is a God of opportunity, a God of season, a God who turns mourning into dancing. He's the God who takes the spirit of heaviness and gives us the garment of praise. He is the God who knows how to take weeping that endures for the long nights and turn that weeping around so that joy comes in the morning. Hallelujah!

Father, I bless your people. I bless those who uniquely need to hear this word. I know that the preaching and teaching of your Word always releases inspiration and hope and encouragement to people. By the power of the Holy Spirit, send this word to give them life.

I pray in the name of Jesus that according to the word of the Lord, the devil would not come and devour this seed, that it would not fall upon places of weeds and get choked out. I pray this word will not fall upon stony places where it cannot take root, that it will not be in places too shallow to flourish without having deep roots. I declare that this word shall fall upon good ground and that those who hear it shall receive it and that it shall become part of their lives and produce fruit.

I pray for the fruit of endurance. Somebody reading this feels tired, weary, and like giving up. They feel like *Lord, if it's one more thing, I don't know if I can take it. God, if I have to deal with just one more circumstance, one more situation, Lord, I'm doing all that I know to do. I don't know what else to do, Father.* So, I pray strength for that person in the name of Jesus. I pray for those who feel hopeless and helpless. I declare that the help of the Lord is going to come to them.

God, give them strategy and insight, give them wisdom to dig themselves out of the pit. Give them the wherewithal to find their way out of the darkness that has been accompanying them, surrounding them, and canopying their life. That darkness has been so thick. Lord, with your machete, cut that darkness. Shed a light and released them from the heaviness, depression, despair, and discouragement in Jesus's mighty name.

Father may the Holy Spirit descend upon the person reading this whose heart is heavy, who may be wiping tears from their eyes even now as the Holy Spirit is beginning to work. I pray in the mighty name of Jesus that you would allow the power of the blood of Jesus to touch the hearts and the lives of your people.

Lord, fear is not our portion. People may forget us. Managers and bosses may forget us. Those who made promises to us of what they're going to do and how they're going to do it and why they are going to do it, they may forget us, Father. Well-meaning people may forget us. Those who have power may forget us, but Lord, I am thankful that you are God and never forgets us! You are with us!

---

Father may the Holy Spirit descend upon
the person reading this whose heart is
heavy, who may be wiping tears from their
eyes even now as the Holy Spirit is
beginning to work.

---

Lord, just as Cornelius, the first Gentile to be baptized in the Holy Spirit, had an angelic visitation, and told him that his prayers and good works had come up like a memorial before the Lord, remind your people, God, that their prayers and good works are going up like memorials. At the right time, and in the right season, when the moment is right, God, turn things around for the one reading these words, in Jesus's name.

May each one not despair, not get frustrated to the point of wanting to quit. May they stay resilient and make it in Jesus's name! Amen.

# Chapter 4:
## Joseph and God's Plan (Forgiveness)

"Forgiveness is a very difficult topic and not for the faint of heart."

## Introduction – The Mother Emanuel AME Church Shooting

On June 17, 2015, the nation was rocked with news of a shocking domestic terrorist. A young man, motivated by racism and with a heart filled with hate, walked into the sacred space of the Emanuel AME Church in Charleston, SC. While the saints were in Bible Study, they sincerely welcomed this young man into their fellowship. He opened fire, causing nine fatalities, including the Lead Pastor, Rev. Clem Pinckney.

At the young man's trial, these words were spoken by the survivors' family:[1]

- "I forgive you," Nadine Collier, the daughter of 70-year-old Ethel Lance, said at the hearing, her voice breaking with emotion. "You took something very precious from me. I will never talk to her again. I will never, ever hold her again. But I forgive you. And have mercy on your soul."

---

[1] Mark Berman, "'I Forgive You.' Relatives of Charleston Church Shooting Victims Address Dylann Roof," Washington Post, June 19, 2015, accessed July 8, 2021, https://www.washingtonpost.com/news/post-nation/wp/2015/06/19/i-forgive-you-relatives-of-charleston-church-victims-address-dylann-roof/.

- "We welcomed you Wednesday night in our Bible study with welcome arms," said Felicia Sanders, her voice trembling. Felicia Sanders was the mother of Tywanza Sanders, who was killed. "Tywanza Sanders was my son. But Tywanza Sanders was my hero. Tywanza was my hero. … May God have mercy on you."

It was a horrific trial. I remember when it happened. That church was nicknamed "Mother Emmanuel Church" because it served as the mother church for the AME movement, which was started as the first African American, independent denomination by ex-slaves. Now, I don't think this young man knew the historic significance of Mother Emmanuel Church, but the enemy knew, and this young man was led there to do damage that night.

## Joseph Forgives His Brothers

"Then Joseph could not restrain himself before all those who stood by him, and he cried out, 'Make everyone go out from me!' So, no one stood with him while Joseph made himself known to his brothers. And he wept aloud, and the Egyptians and the house of Pharaoh heard it. Then Joseph said to his brothers, 'I am Joseph; does my father still live?' But his brothers could not answer him, for they were dismayed in his presence."

"And Joseph said to his brothers, 'Please come near to me.' So, they came near. Then he said: 'I am Joseph your brother, whom you sold into Egypt. But now, do not therefore be grieved or angry with yourselves because you sold me here; for God sent me before you to preserve life. For these two years the famine has been in the land, and there are still five years in which there will be neither plowing nor harvesting. And God sent me before you to preserve a posterity for you in the earth, and to save your lives by a great deliverance'" (Gen 45:1-7).

In Genesis 45:1-7, we see Joseph forgiving his brothers. Through actions he was not responsible for, his brothers set in motion a series of events that were not without consequence. Their decisions and actions caused Joseph to endure hard things, hard places, difficult seasons, and face tough circumstances and situations.

Now we find Joseph ruling in Egypt. The dream, the promise that God gave him as a young man has now come to pass. Up to the point when Joseph could not restrain himself and cried out, his brothers did not know he was Joseph. They did not realize that this was the young man they threw in the pit those years ago. He looked like an Egyptian. He was speaking in the Egyptian tongue. He has aged, matured. The young man they threw in the pit now is a grown man with power. We see in this story Joseph's pain, his brothers' plot, but the Lord's plan.

## Joseph's Pain

"[H]e wept aloud, and the Egyptians and the house of Pharaoh heard it." Joseph has what is known a cathartic moment, when all those emotions which he has been carrying get released out of his soul.

So, when Joseph couldn't take it anymore, couldn't restrain himself, the Bible says that he sent everyone out—all his attendants, workers, staff members—so that no one stood with Joseph while he made himself known to his brothers. He weeps aloud, and the Bible says that the Egyptians and the house of Pharoah hear it. This was not Joseph just having cute tears trickling down the side of his face. Joseph was carrying grief beyond measure. I believe that everything came back to him in this moment—all he had endured and gone through. The fear, animosity, anxiety, worry, stress, discouragement, frustration—every single toxic emotion he had experienced—all came back to him in that moment, so much so that Pharaoh and all the Egyptians there heard him weep aloud.

"And Joseph said to his brothers, 'I am Joseph.'" He goes on to communicate his concern, "Does my father still live?" He wants to know if his dad was still alive; they had deprived him of all those years of being with him. However, his brothers could not answer, the Bible says, because they were dismayed in his presence.

---

Joseph weeps aloud and the house of
Pharoah hears it. This was not Joseph just
having cute tears trickling down the side of
his face. Joseph was carrying
grief beyond measure.

---

Think about this. They know exactly what they did to Joseph. And if you have read the text, you know that prior to revealing himself here in Genesis 45, Joseph dealt with them pretty sternly. He has been pretty difficult to deal with, trying to get them to understand that he wants to get his younger brother, Benjamin, there. He finally gets Benjamin there, and he wants to get his father there. So finally, when he reveals himself, they don't know how to respond. They don't know what their brother is going to do to them.

Joseph says to his brothers, "Please come near to me." So, they come near, and he says to them again, "I am Joseph, your brother." I love that.

"I am Joseph, your brother, who you sold into Egypt. But now
don't be grieved or angry with yourselves because you sold me.
I see God had a plan in all of this. God sent me here to preserve
a life, for these two years famine that has been in the land and
there's still five more years which is yet to be, there'll be
nothing to plow and nothing to harvest. God sent me
before you to preserve a posterity in the earth and to
save your lives by a great deliverance" (Gen 45:1-7)

He says, "God sent me to preserve your life." Notice, Joseph does not marginalize his pain. The pain he felt was real, authentic, and sincere. He wept so loud that the Egyptians and even Pharaoh's house around him wept. When you've been injured, wronged, taken advantage of, and manipulated, when you only meant good, and folks paid you evil for the good you've done, it *hurts*. It's *painful*. Notice, Joseph is not in denial. He's not just marginalizing how he feels. *He embraces his emotions.* Hear me. *He deals with the reality of his feelings.*

---

Joseph is not in denial. He doesn't marginalize how he feels. *He embraces his emotions. He deals with the reality of his feelings.*

---

Joseph has what is known by therapists as a cathartic moment. All those emotions he had been carrying get released out of his soul and gets expressed through the vehicle of his physical body—the tears, screaming, weeping, and moaning. Hear me, when you have been injured and wronged, you need these cathartic moments to be freed of these toxic, negative emotions.

One of the most beautiful sights to witness as a spiritual leader are those cathartic moments around the altar where people can come and have a safe place with spiritual people laying hands on one another, to release emotions and let go of grief and pain.

Joseph had all these emotions bottled up inside of him, and when he reveals himself to his brothers, he sends everyone away because he knows it's not going to be pretty. I don't mean he was angry or ugly or mean; I'm saying he knew that raw emotion was going to come out of him. Sometimes we get so caught up in spiritual things that we neglect our soul's health, our physical health, and our emotional health by bottling things up and holding things in. We don't understand how to have these cathartic moments where we let these things go.

Joseph had his cathartic moment where those emotions got purged out of him. That's the thing I missed the most during Covid, because I know that the altar is where we have these cathartic moments— when you walk up to a deacon, an elder, another spiritual leader, even a brother or sister, and they look you in the eye and say, "How can I pray for you?" There's something about hearing those words and feeling the touch of someone laying hands upon you, experiencing the release of the anointing and the power of the Spirit from person to person, releasing those toxic, negative emotions in us.

Joseph had carried all this stuff—the betrayal, the falsehood, the pain—and it all culminated in that moment.

## The Brothers' Plot

"I am Joseph your brother, whom you sold into Egypt." Joseph acknowledges the past. He doesn't pretend as if it didn't occur, nor does he minimize what happened. He recognizes, embraces, and verbalizes what happened. He acknowledges the fact that his brothers plotted and schemed all of this.

One of the most painful things about what these brothers did was not only that they sold Joseph into slavery, but that they came back home and reported to their father, saying to him, "Joseph was killed." Hearing the father say, "I will mourn for Joseph for the rest of my life," and watching the old man day by day, week by week, month by month, year after year after year, seeing how his grief and anguish of calling to Joseph is so painful to read about. Jacob did not have his cathartic moment all that time He was carrying these emotions. He already had to bury a wife who died giving childbirth to Joseph's younger brother, Benjamin. Now he has to live with the reality of the fact that his beloved son is dead. His other sons knew this for years and years and said *nothing* to their father. What a wicked thing they did.

Joseph acknowledges to them, "The reason I'm here is because of what you did. I'm your brother who you sold to Egypt. This is what *you did*. It makes no sense trying to sugarcoat it. You sold me like I was a cow, an ox, a sheep, or a lamb. You sold me like I was a *thing*, but I'm not a thing. I'm a human being, I'm a person, and not only am I a person, but I'm also your *brother*. And this is what you did." So, Joseph acknowledges the past. He doesn't pretend like it didn't occur, and he doesn't minimize what happened. He recognizes, embraces, and verbalizes the truth of what happened.

---



---

Forgiveness is not about just forgetting what happened. Part of forgiveness is having a cathartic moment where you let it go, acknowledging what went on between us. You hurt me. You plotted, you planned, I overheard your conversation; you were going to kill me, and it was Reuben who said, "Let's not kill him. Let's sell him because there is no profit in his blood. So, let's at least make a profit from it. I overheard that conversation while I was in the pit. I overheard you plotting and scheming and strategizing against me. So, let's not pretend that didn't happen."

Joseph has this moment of pain, this cathartic moment. He recognizes the past, but he also acknowledges the Lord's plan.

## The Lord's Plan

"God sent me before you to preserve life. ... And God sent me before you to preserve a posterity for you in the earth, and to save your lives by a great deliverance." Joseph acknowledges that amid his pain and the scheme, the Lord had a plan. God's plan was to preserve posterity and save lives.

He says, "God sent me before you. Now, I don't know how God would have gotten me here if y'all hadn't done this wickedness, but the Lord would have had a way. The Lord would have done what He had planned for my life. But I see now, as I look back, the hand of God, the providential work of God in my life. God sent me before you to preserve posterity in the earth and to save your lives. Your children and grandchildren are going to benefit from me now being in Egypt." Think about that. What if Joseph had failed at Potiphar's house? What if Joseph had failed in the prison? What if Joseph had felt like he was forgotten? It would have skewed God's plan, but because he kept himself in a place where the Lord could continue to use him, now he was at a point where he could say, "I see the hand of God over your life."

---

Because Joseph kept himself in a place
where the Lord could continue to use him,
now he was at a point where he could say,
"I see the hand of God over your life."

---

I see the plan of God working. So, Joseph had his **pain**, acknowledging the **past**, but third, he recognizes that God had a **plan**—to preserve their posterity and save lives.

Listen, amid your betrayals, hurts, wounds, and all the deeds that have injured you, God has had a plan. I know you have your pain. I know it's easy to get stuck in the past, but you have to deal with the third P, that God has a plan.

# What Exactly is Forgiveness?

The best definition I have heard for forgiveness is, "me giving up my right to hurt you for hurting me." I may feel that I have a right to hurt back the one who wronged me, but forgiveness says, I'm going to suspend my right. I'm going to deny my right to hurt you because you hurt me. That's what forgiveness is.

According to an article from the Mayo Clinic, forgiveness is "a decision to let go of resentment and thoughts of revenge."[2] Forgiveness involves every part of our humanity—spirit, soul, mind, will, and body.

Forgiveness is a decision. Forgiveness is not just something emotional. It might express itself in an emotional manner, but forgiveness does not orient or originate in the emotions. One of the most untrustworthy things you can rely on is your emotions because one minute you're happy, and one minute, you're sad. If you look outside and it's gray, then you get gray in your spirit. If the sun is shining, you get happy, right? Forgiveness begins in the will.

Forgiveness is a posture of the soul. It's a decision that I'm going to let go of resentment and will not seek revenge after you. The opposite of forgiveness is being unforgiving—carrying resentment and thoughts of revenge. Unforgiveness means you're going to embrace the right to hurt you for hurting me. I'm not trying to minimize any pain you have had to endure—whether infidelity of a spouse, someone stealing something from you, or someone violating you in a particular way. No matter how you have been hurt or injured, hear me child of God, the Lord wants you to forgive because

---

[2] Mayo Clinic Staff, "Forgiveness: Letting Go of Grudges and Bitterness," Mayo Clinic (Healthy Lifestyle, Adult Health), accessed July 8, 2021, https://www.mayoclinic.org/healthy-lifestyle/adult-health/in-depth/forgiveness/art-20047692.

forgiveness impacts every part of our humanity. It affects your spirit, soul, mind, will, and body.

# Why Forgive?

"The heart knows its own bitterness"
(Prov 14:10, NKJV).

Proverbs 14:10 says, "Every heart knows its own bitterness." I don't know what you've been through. You don't know what I've been through. I may talk about what I've experienced, but we really don't get into the gut emotion of it most of the time. Everybody knows that. You know what's made you bitter in life, and I have things that could try to make me bitter. Still, we need to forgive—but *why*?

## Forgiveness is a Spiritual Principle

First, forgiveness is a spiritual principle. It's not emotional. It's got to be spiritual. What do I mean? **We serve a God who forgives us.** That thing that says forgiveness is me giving up the right to hurt you for hurting me, you know, God says that every day. Darnell, you did this thing that hurt me, and I could get you. Some people have a theology of a God that He's out to get you. You are constantly looking over your shoulder thinking the Lord is going to pay you back evil for evil. That's not the God we serve. We serve a God who practices forgiveness. Hear what he says: "For you O Lord, You are ready to forgive" (Ps 86:5). Isn't that wonderful? He is a God who is ready to forgive. He's good. He's abundant in mercy to those who call upon His name. He's ready to forgive.

Not only is he a God who forgives, but also, **He is a God who has commanded us to be forgiving**. He has commanded it! Yes, every heart knows his own bitterness, and sometimes your pain can become so frequent and so familiar that you can't imagine a life without having that pain. But we serve a God who not only forgives, but He also calls us to *be* forgiving! When the Lord taught us to pray,

He said, "Our father who art in heaven, hallowed be thy name, thy kingdom come. Thy will be done on earth as it is in heaven. Give us this day, our daily bread and forgive us as we forgive those who have trespassed against us" (Matt 6:9-12). Forgive us *as* we forgive. He goes on in verses 14-15, "For if you forgive men their trespasses, your heavenly Father will also forgive you. But if you do not forgive men their trespasses, neither will your Father forgive your trespasses."

You should pray the Lord's Prayer every day of your life. If that's not a part of your talking to God, begin to incorporate it on your way to work. As you brush your teeth, as you're having a cup of coffee, quote the Lord's Prayer. Find a way to plug it into your life every day. Hear what He says: "Forgive us *as* we forgive." In other words, when we pray this prayer, we are saying to the Lord, "I recognize that for me to be fully forgiven by you, I have to forgive those that hurt me." That's powerful, saints—powerful!

Again, I'm not minimizing your pain. I'm not asking you to ignore your past. I do want you to see that God has a plan. I want you to understand that we serve a God who is ready to forgive and who commands us to forgive.

Why forgive? The third reason is that **the Lord Jesus modeled a life of forgiveness for us**. I was with some Bible school students once, and they were asking me, "Dr. Williams, how do you define success in ministry?" And I said, "You have to be very careful with that because you can't use human markers of success. There are some who are successful by human standards, but they are failures in God's eyes. And there are some who are failures in the eyes of people but very successful in God's eyes." I said, "If you look at Jesus, the moment of His life that seems to be his greatest failure, was, in fact, the most successful moment of His life, when He was dying on the Cross." His assignment in that moment is to die, but He stops dying to pray a prayer, "Father, forgive them for they don't know what they're doing" (Luke 23:34). Father, *forgive* them. He stops long enough from dying to offer forgiveness to those who wronged Him.

So, there are three *spiritual* reasons why we forgive: we serve a God who forgives, He commands us to forgive, and He even modeled forgiveness for us. That's what I love about Jesus. Jesus doesn't tell us to live one way then He commands us to do something else. He lived it; He modeled the right way for us.

## Forgiveness Benefits Us

"Unforgiveness is like drinking poison yourself and waiting for the other person to die." —Marianne Williamson

There are also '*selfish* reasons' why we forgive—because forgiveness benefits us! When I say that, I'm using air quotes around 'selfish reasons.' Why? Because forgiveness is to your benefit and one of the best measures of self-care you can undertake.

Marianne Williamson says, "Unforgiveness is like drinking poison yourself and waiting for the other person to die." You have not hurt the other person by your unforgiveness. You have only hurt yourself. Forgive—not just for *spiritual* reasons, but for *selfish* reasons.

The Mayo Clinic article also describes several benefits of forgiveness:[3]

- Healthier relationships
- Improved mental health.
- Less anxiety, stress and hostility
- Lower blood pressure
- Fewer symptoms of depression
- A stronger immune system
- Improved heart health
- Improved self-esteem

---

[3] Ibid.

- First, when you practice forgiveness, you have healthier relationships.

- Second, when you practice forgiveness, you have improved mental health. See, it affects us, body, soul, mind, and spirit. So, forgiveness is not just about bearing under the weight of some command that I've been wronged, and I want to immerse myself in my grief and my pain. It affects so many areas of my life. When you forgive, you're going to improve your mental health.

- Third, you have less anxiety, stress, and hostility in your life when you practice forgiveness. Fourth, being a forgiving person can actually lower your blood pressure!

- Fifth, the symptoms of depression will start to diminish as you forgive.

- Sixth, you develop a stronger immune system when you forgive. Did you know that?

- You also have improved heart health and better self-esteem when you practice forgiveness.

I would add having a clear and clean conscience before God and others, too. Priceless! There is nothing to be compared with a clear and clean conscience before God and others; it's priceless. Knowing you have a good standing with God and others is priceless. There's no value you can place on a clear conscience before God and men.

> There is nothing to be compared with a
> clear and clean conscience before God
> and others.

I know you may be suffering, and I know someone may have wronged you. I know the pain is still there, but you can forgive for selfish (i.e., self-care) reasons.

## Joseph Really, Really, Really Forgave Them

> When Joseph's brothers saw that their father was dead, they said, "Perhaps Joseph will hate us, and may actually repay us for all the evil which we did to him." So, they sent messengers to Joseph, saying, "Before your father died, he commanded, saying, 'Thus you shall say to Joseph: "I beg you, please forgive the trespass of your brothers and their sin; for they did evil to you."'" "Now, please, forgive the trespass of the servants of the God of your father." And Joseph wept when they spoke to him. Then his brothers also went and fell down before his face, and they said, "Behold, we [are] your servants." Joseph said to them, "Do not be afraid, for am I in the place of God? But as for you, you meant evil against me; but God meant it for good, in order to bring it about as it is this day, to save many people alive. Now therefore, do not be afraid; I will provide for you and your little ones." And he comforted them and spoke kindly to them (Gen 50:15).

I know sometimes you want to say, "God, get them," but "'Vengeance is mine,' says the Lord. 'I'll deal with them. You just forgive them. You let it go'" (Deut 32:35; Rom 12:19).

Joseph *really* forgave his brothers. Joseph's forgiveness was raw and real. It was authentic. So, you know the story. The brothers go, they get Jacob, they send back a caravan. Jacob is there, and they tell him, "Joseph is alive. Our brother is alive." Jacob says, "Y'all lying to me. You told me years ago Joseph was dead. Now, you're going to tell me he's alive. I don't believe you." And the Bible says when he saw the wagons, it says that the spirit of Jacob came alive again. Jacob had been carrying a grief, a huge loss.

Now he gets his own cathartic moment! Jacob gets to purge the toxic emotions from his soul. His sons bring him down to Egypt and he meets Joseph and Joseph's children—Ephraim and Manasseh. We hear the story of how he blesses them by crossing his arms over their heads as they kneel before him. And then Jacob dies.

Genesis 50:15 says, "But Joseph's brothers saw that their father had died." They were manipulative. They always thought they were smarter than everybody else, trying to hustle people and get the advantage. So, they whisper to each other, "Perhaps Joseph will hate us and may actually repay us for the evil we did to him." They felt insecure. They probably thought, *well, maybe Joseph was doing this nice-guy stuff until our father dies, then he's going to get us.* Kind of like what Michael in *The Godfather* does to this brother: "As long as mom is alive, you get to stay alive. But when mama's gone, you are going to get your end. I'm going to pay you back for betraying me." That wasn't the case, but that was what they thought, that perhaps Joseph would pay them back for the evil they did.

So, they go to Joseph's messengers and concoct a story: "You know, before your father died, not our father, *your* father, before your father died, he commanded—we don't know if you got this message or not—but *he commanded* that we tell you something. And here's what Dad said, Joseph: 'I beg you, forgive the trespasses of your brothers and their sins for they did evil to you.'" Now they're lying, of course. Jacob never said this, but they are in fear that Joseph now will somehow exact revenge upon them from resentment he's been nursing.

Joseph's brothers fall down on their faces before him and beg him, saying, "We are your servants."

I want you to hear this; Joseph *really* forgave them. He says to them, "Do not be afraid, for I am in the place of God?" In other words, "I've dealt with this so long ago, guys, this is already done. This is a closed issue for me. If there's anything else that's going to be left to deal with this, God himself is going to have to do it." He says, "But as for you, I know you meant it for evil against me, but God meant it for good, in order to bring about the thing that's happened this day to save many people alive." And he adds, "Now therefore don't be afraid. I will provide for you and your little ones." And he *comforted* them and *spoke kindly* to them. Joseph *really* forgave them.

## Final Thoughts

When you've been wronged or hurt, human nature connects emotion to events. Not long ago, I was talking about my mother and telling a story about her, and I found myself starting to tear up because the moment of her death was a strong emotional moment for me. It still invokes emotion. We connect emotion to thinking about events; that's just the way we're wired.

You may be in a place where you're experiencing pain right now. You know you need to forgive, but you're saying, "Lord, it still hurts." Well, that hurt is the emotion that's connected to the memory of that moment when you were violated, abused, misused, taken advantage of, exploited, stolen from, and on and on. So please don't think that because the emotion is there that it prevents you from extending forgiveness. If you forgive, the emotion will start to connect to the act of forgiveness that's going to override that current emotion. You understand what I'm saying? Because you still hurt, please don't let that keep you from extending forgiveness.

I have described this in a technical way, but here's a practical way to look at it. If I go outside and someone runs their car over my foot and crushes my toe, and they jump out and say, "Oh, Bishop! I'm sorry! I didn't mean to do this!" I will forgive you—but it still hurts.

There's a scene in *The Lion King* when Rafiki is talking to Simba, and he pops him on the head and says, "It's all in the past, it's all in the past." Simba rubbing his head, says, "Yeah, but the past still hurts." For some of us, the past still hurts. I get it. Seek the Lord for a cathartic moment.

Please understand, I'm not here to minimize your pain or give you a shallow coping mechanism. I'm leading you to still waters to restore your soul, to the well where you can pick up your joy again.

There are some people you need to let go. You are carrying them in your spirit, and they've gone on with their life. They don't even remember what they did to you. You're not even part of that conversation anymore, but you're still living with it and nursing that hurt. I want to challenge you to just let them go free.

I know some of us have personality types where we feel like things are left undone until we could sit across from the person and say, "I need to tell you what you did to me and how you made me feel." But sometimes you just won't get that opportunity. I was talking to a young lady who had her heart broken by a young man. She was in tears talking to me, saying, "I need to talk to him and tell him." I said, "You know what? You may not need to talk to him. Here's what I'm going to tell you to do. Maybe you need to write him a letter and get all that emotion out of you. Then go to the kitchen and go to the stove and burn that letter so nobody ever reads it." There's something about getting toxic emotions out!

Another thing to remember is that there is a difference between forgiveness and trust. Forgiving someone does not necessarily mean that we have to trust them as we did before. Please let us not confuse forgiveness and a shift in relational dynamics. Trust is something that is earned. Once trust is violated, it often has to be rebuilt, one moment at a time.

Forgiveness is a complex and complicated issue. If you need to explore the topic more, there are plenty of resources written by people of faith who explore the topic in far more detail than we do here. Likewise, if you are struggling to forgive someone, seek out pastoral counseling as well as some biblical based therapy.

## Prayer

Father, I thank you, Lord, that every day we're reminded that you are a God who forgives. You tell us to forgive others and that as we do, you, our heavenly Father, will forgive us. Lord, some people reading this book may have gone through sexual violation—maybe molestation as a child, rape, or some kind of sexual abuse. Some may have been talked about, lied about, or maybe went through a divorce and the old spouse just hurt them so badly that they've been carrying around that pain for years.

Maybe someone experienced having something stolen from them, they were taken advantage of, exploited, treated badly by a sibling or a parent. Holy Spirit, I invite you to come and just move in the heart of your child.

This is a weighty subject, Lord, but you can do your work in each one. I pray that as we've looked at the life of Joseph, that this will be a template for others to challenge themselves, to be people who will forgive. Your Word tells us that as high as the heavens are above the earth, so great is your mercy toward them that fear you. As far as the east is from the west, so far have you removed our transgressions from us. Your Word says that like a father pity his children, so the Lord pities those who fear Him.

Father, I pray for the balm of Gilead to come upon the one reading these words. I pray that anger, resentment, and unforgiveness harbored in the heart for so long will be set free in the name of Jesus. Holy Spirit, please do a work in this person, and may he or she experience the healing of the Lord.

I pray Lord that not only will these natural and physiological things resolve, but that Lord, your joy and peace would return. I even pray for those having difficulty forgiving themselves, walking in guilt and shame. Lord, help that one let themselves go in forgiveness as well because you are the God who gives hope.

Father, I invite you to come and do a work. Help us, O God, to be people who are merciful and who forgive others who have wronged them. Thank you for helping us forgive. I give you praise, honor, and glory in Jesus's name. Amen.

# Conclusion

You know, the older I get, I see the value of having a coach in life. Sometimes you need therapy and counseling that can help us. When I was young and cavalier, I had a lot of zeal, but not all the knowledge. I had a lot of fire in my heart, but I didn't have a lot of wisdom in my head. I just felt like prayer answered everything, and I would just confess everything. But you know what? Now I've come to realize that God uses counselors who understand how the Lord has made the mind work, and how the mind, body, spirit, soul, heart, and will interconnect.

So, if you don't know what to do, if you want to forgive, but feel stuck and don't know how to move forward, reach out to a trusted counselor. If you want to read a great book on forgiveness, R. C. Sproul wrote a book called *Total Forgiveness*. And there are other great Christian resources out there.

Thank you for taking this Joseph journey with me. We talked about betrayal. We talked about the collision of favor and falsehood. We talked about being forgotten. And we talked about Joseph and forgiveness.

God bless you!

# About the Author

Dr. Darnell K. Williams, Sr.

**Beginnings.** A native of Cleveland, Ohio, Darnell grew up in a single parent home. With an incredible support system, lots of determination, and the grace of God, he was able to push beyond the pains of his childhood and pursue God's plan for his life. Dr. Darnell accepted Christ at sixteen years old and began ministry at nineteen.

**Ministry.** He was ordained to the gospel ministry in 1992. Currently, He is the Associate Professor of Pastoral Studies, College of Church Leadership, North Central University, Minneapolis, MN.

From 2006-2022, he served as senior pastor of One Church Lima, (formerly New Life Church International) a multiethnic church in Lima, Ohio.

He holds an ordination credential with the Assemblies of God.

**Education.** He holds an earned Doctor of Ministry from the Assemblies of God Theological Seminary in Springfield, MO.

**Professionally.** His business background spans the areas of banking, credit cards, mortgages, and insurance.

**Publications.** Dr. Darnell authored the book, *Wings to Rise: Blacks, Leadership, and the Assemblies of God* in 2020 and has published numerous articles.

**Leadership.** Dr. Darnell has served as

- Secretary-Treasurer of the International Ministry Network (German District) of the Assemblies of God (2014-2020)

- Vice President of the National Black Fellowship of the Assemblies of God

- General Presbyter of the Assemblies of God (by virtue of office, 2014-current)

- Executive Presbyter of the Assemblies of God (elected at the 58th General Council)

In 2012, Williams was consecrated to the office of Bishop. Serving with his wife, Pastor K. Charlene, they provide coaching, consulting, and apostolic oversight.

**Community.** Dr. Darnell served in the following capacities:

- President of Judah Enterprises, non-profit ministry that provided outreach to families facing food insecurities and ministering compassion to those in need

- Rhodes State College University Foundation Board

- Trustee for Evangel University

- Chaplain for Lima Memorial health systems

- Chaplain of the Lima Police Department.

**Family.** Dr. Darnell has been happily married (since 1993) to his beautiful wife, Kim Charlene, of Georgetown Guyana, South America. She serves alongside him in ministry. They are the proud parents of one son, Adrian, who is completing a MD/PhD program.

* 9 7 9 8 8 6 9 0 3 4 1 1 3 *